Teacher Resource Book

GRADE 1

CONCORDIA PUBLISHING HOUSE • SAINT LOUIS

3558 S. Jefferson Avenue, St. Louis, MO 63118-3968
1-800-325-3040 • www.cph.org

Written by Christine Behnke, Corey Brandenburger, Susan Brandt, Sylvia Bronner, Chad Bryant, Lindsey Burken, Lori Christiansen, Erin Dueck, Ruth Geisler, Drew Gerdes, Kriss Glaeser, Jane Haas, Patricia A. Hoffman, Chrissy Iadarola, Rachel Kuehner, Gail Marsh, Diane Maurer, Heather Meyer, Roxy Mueller, Judy Norton, Deanna Sandcork, Carolyn Sims, Anita Stohs, Diane Tinker, Kari Vo, Marian Weber, Marilyn Wiesehan

Edited by Lorraine Groth, Gail Pawlitz, Brenda Trunkhill

Series editors: Rodney L. Rathmann, Carolyn Bergt, Brenda Trunkhill

Editorial assistant: Amanda G. Lansche

Manufactured in the United States of America

Preface

This *Teacher Resource Book* is divided into nine units that correspond with the nine units of the One in Christ Student Book and Teacher Guide. Each unit will contain a list of the memory work for the unit, a parent letter, and unit assessment ideas. These pages will be followed by the lesson reproducible pages for that same unit. To avoid an abundance of numbers, no page numbers are listed. Instead, you will find the unit number at the top of the introductory pages, and the numbers of the lesson reproducibles will be found at the bottom corner of the page. (Answers for these activities are found in the minimized version presented in the Teacher Guide lessons.) At the end of the book, you will find worship resources (prayers, psalms, and music) to use as you see fit; however, we suggest that the puppet skits are most appropriate for use at the beginning of the year, to introduce worship concepts.

All of the pages in this *Teacher Resource Book* are also available as downloads from the One in Christ Web site. The pages are provided in these two formats so that you can choose the method that is more convenient for you. May God bless you as you use these materials to teach children about their Lord and Savior Jesus Christ!

Glossary

- **altar** An important tablelike church furnishing used in worship.
- **ark** (1) The boat God told Noah to build. (2) The gold box that carried reminders that God was with the people of Israel.
- **believe** To trust and be certain something or someone is true.
- **blessing** A gift from God.
- **disciple** A follower of Jesus.
- **eternal** Never ending.
- **faith** Trusting in your heart that Jesus forgives and saves you.
- **Gospel** The Good News that Jesus died on the cross and arose on Easter for us.
- **grace** The kindness of God, which, as sinners, we do not deserve.
- **heaven** Where we will live with God eternally because of Jesus.
- **holy** Without sin.
- **Jesus** The promised Messiah, Savior of the world, the Christ, our Lord, the Son of God, and the King of kings.
- **mercy** Pity and compassion for those who suffer.
- **praise** To say or sing good things about someone.
- **rejoice** To be glad or celebrate.
- **repent** To admit and be sorry about your sin; to turn to God in faith in Jesus and receive His forgiveness, and through His help to turn away from sin and live as God's child.
- **resurrection** Coming back to life after death.
- **serve** To willingly and humbly do kind things to help others.
- **shepherd** Someone who watches over and cares for sheep.
- **tempt** To lead someone to do wrong.
- **witness** To tell what you know to be true.
- **worship** To receive God's Word in faith and to respond with prayer, praise, and thanksgiving.

Unit 1

Words to Remember

1. I praise You, for I am . . . wonderfully made. Wonderful are Your works.
   Psalm 139:14
2. The one who is in you is greater than the one who is in the world. 1 John 4:4 NIV
3. God is our refuge and strength, a very present help in trouble. Psalm 46:1
4. I trust in You, O LORD; I say, "You are my God." Psalm 31:14
5. Faith is being sure of what we hope for and certain of what we do not see.
   Hebrews 11:1 NIV
6. Repent, then, and turn to God, so that your sins may be wiped out. Acts 3:19 NIV
7. We know that for those who love God all things work together for good. Romans 8:28
8. You did not choose Me, but I chose you."
   John 15:16

Dear Parents,

In the next few weeks, as we learn more about God's love, we will study how God blesses families. Your child will study Adam and Eve, Cain and Abel; Noah and his sons; Abraham, Sarah, and Isaac; Isaac and Rebekah, Jacob and Esau; Joseph and his brothers; Moses, his mother, and sister, Miriam.

As students learn about families in the Bible, they will see many similarities with their own families—yours and the Church family—including sin and conflict. Most importantly, students will see how God is gracious and merciful to His children. God knows what is best for His children and even uses those bad things that happen to us for good. Your child will see the depth of our heavenly Father's love for His children through the blessing of His Son, Jesus, as our Savior. God abundantly blesses His children with all that they need to live here on earth and for eternity with Him in heaven. "He who did not spare His own Son but gave Him up for us all, how will He not also with Him graciously give us all things?" (Romans 8:32).

Read the Bible stories in *God Blesses a Family* to your child. Consider how God has blessed your family with what you need, especially the need for forgiveness and reconciliation, with each other and with God Himself. May God bless your family's communication, strengthen your relationship with one another, and strengthen your faith to trust that God knows what is best for His children.

Celebrate your adoption into the Church family. God has blessed us with brothers and sisters in Christ to support and encourage each other. When there is conflict in the Church as in any family, pray that the Holy Spirit guides and guards the actions and words of family members.

You will be getting nine of these books throughout the year. Collect these to make one big Bible story book that will show God's loving plan for us through the Old Testament, New Testament, now, and eternally.

Sharing the love of Jesus,
Your child's teacher

Assessment: Unit 1

Students can create a book to show how they recognize that God is with them and cares for them each day. Students can make a book-and-a-half about themselves entitled "God Cares for Me" or "I Am Chosen by God." Take a full-body picture of each child, enlarge and print it twice, then glue it onto two 9 × 12-inch pieces of construction paper. Use the full shot for the back cover, but cut off the top third (the head section) leaving the bottom two-thirds for the front cover. Staple the 8 × 9-inch cover and several 8 × 9-inch story pages (e.g., white construction paper) to the back cover. On the inside pages, students draw their body doing things that show God's blessings (e.g., eating, reading, playing inside and/or outside with or without friends, praying, reading the Bible, and the like). The student's face will stay the same, but as the pages are turned, one different image is shown each time. As they choose poses, students will need to consider how God is with them and cares for them every day and everywhere, just as He was with His people long ago. If students are allowed to use digital cameras and pose in different settings, this could become a multi-media project instead of simply an art project.

Review the Unit 1 Word Wall Words. Encourage students to use as many as they can in journal writing.

As a review throughout the unit or as a culminating project, have students create "Blessing Books." Children use 11 × 17-inch paper, folding the long way and then folding it twice the other way, creating four sections. Starting at the open end, they cut on the three short folds just to the long fold. Students will have created a lift-the-flap story book. To review all the stories, they will need to create two books and tape them together to create one long book of eight sections. On the top flap, students write four or eight (depending on the length of your book) phrases: "God blessed Adam and Eve's family," "God blessed Noah's family," "God blessed Abraham's family," "God blessed Isaac's family," "God blessed Joseph's family," "God blessed Moses' family," "God blessed my family," and "God blessed my school family." (To save time, print these phrases on large labels and just have students attach them.) When the flap is lifted, students draw a picture of that family in the top section. In the bottom section, students complete the phrase using their own words. Possible answers include: "when He created a magnificent world for them to live in," "when He promised a Savior to forgive them of their sins," "when He promised another perfect life and perfect place, in heaven," "when He saved them from destruction," "when He gave them a new start," "when He promised many descendents—including the Savior," "when He brought them to a new land," "when He gave them many physical blessings and made them wealthy," "when He made Jacob a patriarch of His people," "when He helped Joseph to forgive his brothers," "when He made Joseph a blessing to many, helping his family and the entire region to survive a famine," "when He spared Moses' life," "when He made Moses a blessing to many—leading God's people out of slavery." Accept possible answers for how God blessed a student's family or school family. For the final step, the book can be accordion-folded, stacking the pages behind one cover.

Assessment: Unit 1

Give students time to consider how the Lord has a plan for everyone. Ask students to write or say answers to the following questions. What troubles did Joseph have? How did God help Joseph? What troubles did Moses have? How did God help Moses? What troubles do you have? How can God help you? The last two questions are personal, but do point out that their own lives parallel Joseph and Moses'. Reassure the children that God's power and help is there for them too.

Create mobiles for students to draw comparisons between the story of Noah or Abraham and their own story. Have students cut out a cloud pattern from a white piece of construction paper and three large raindrops from blue paper for the Noah story or cut out one large star from yellow construction paper and three smaller stars for the Abraham story. On one side of the large cloud or star, students will write "God's Promises to Abraham" or "Noah." On the other side students will write their own name. Use string and paper clips to attach the three rain drops or smaller stars to the bottom. On one side of the stars or rain drop, students will write a promise God made to Abraham or Noah, and on the other side (when flipped over) students will write a promise God made to him or her. Hang the mobiles so that the promises hang underneath.

After explaining the activity to parents in a note or e-mail home, allow students to use washable markers or face paint to create hand designs. See Web Resource Unit 1a for ideas. Depending on your purpose, assign students specific characters (e.g., animals for the creation or flood stories, modern-day people for life-application stories). Using the Lesson 2, Day 2 "Into the Word" section as an example, give students time to create their own stories with two characters (both hands) interacting. Students will demonstrate their understanding of conflict and forgiveness if you choose modern-day family members and will demonstrate recall of story details if you choose Bible characters. Although the Bible doesn't provide such details, you may want students to tell the Bible story from a different point of view, such as a minor character (e.g., Noah's sons, Noah's neighbors, one of Joseph's brothers, the pharaoh's daughter or her servant, or even an animal in the Garden of Eden or on the ark).

Have students pick one favorite character from the unit to focus on. Students draw a large picture of his face, cut it out, and glue it to the bottom flap of a paper lunch bag. They may add arms out the side (top) of the bag, if desired. Using 3 x 5 – inch lined paper, students write how God blessed that person's family. Staple the paper below the head, aligning the bottom edge of the paper with the bottom edge of the bag. Students can present their thoughts to the class, using the bag as a puppet.

Name: ________________________________

darkness
1
light
heavens
2
water
3
land
trees
flowers
plants
4
sun
stars
moon
5
water creatures
6
birds that fly
7
land animals
8
people
9

Abel

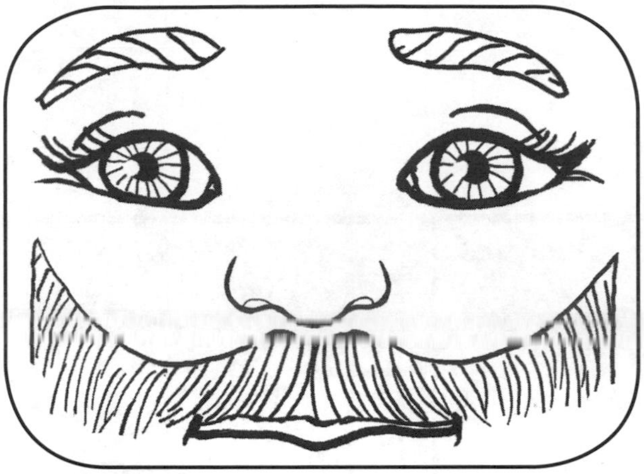

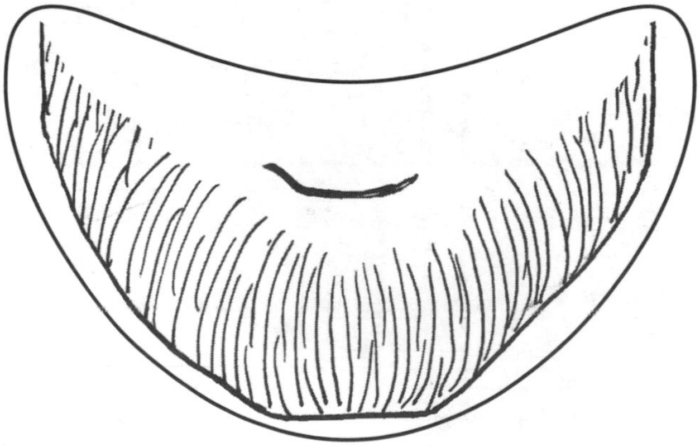

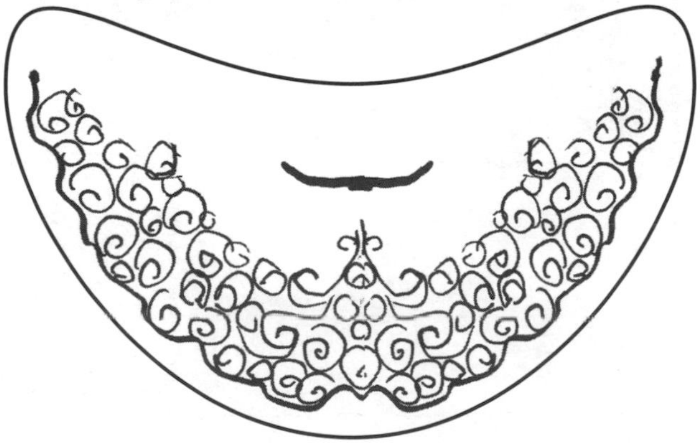

Cain

1.

1.

2.

2.

3.

3.

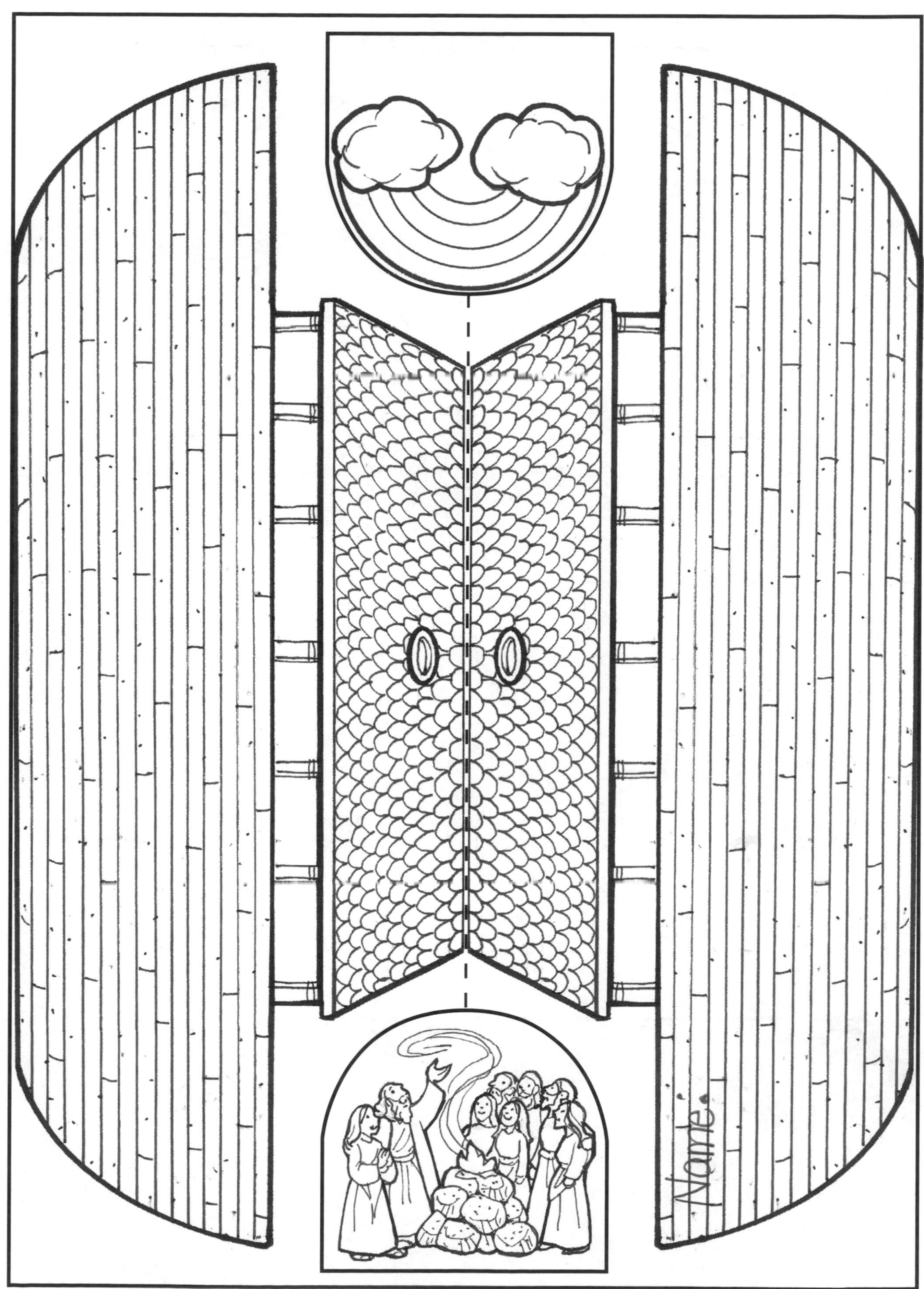

Promises

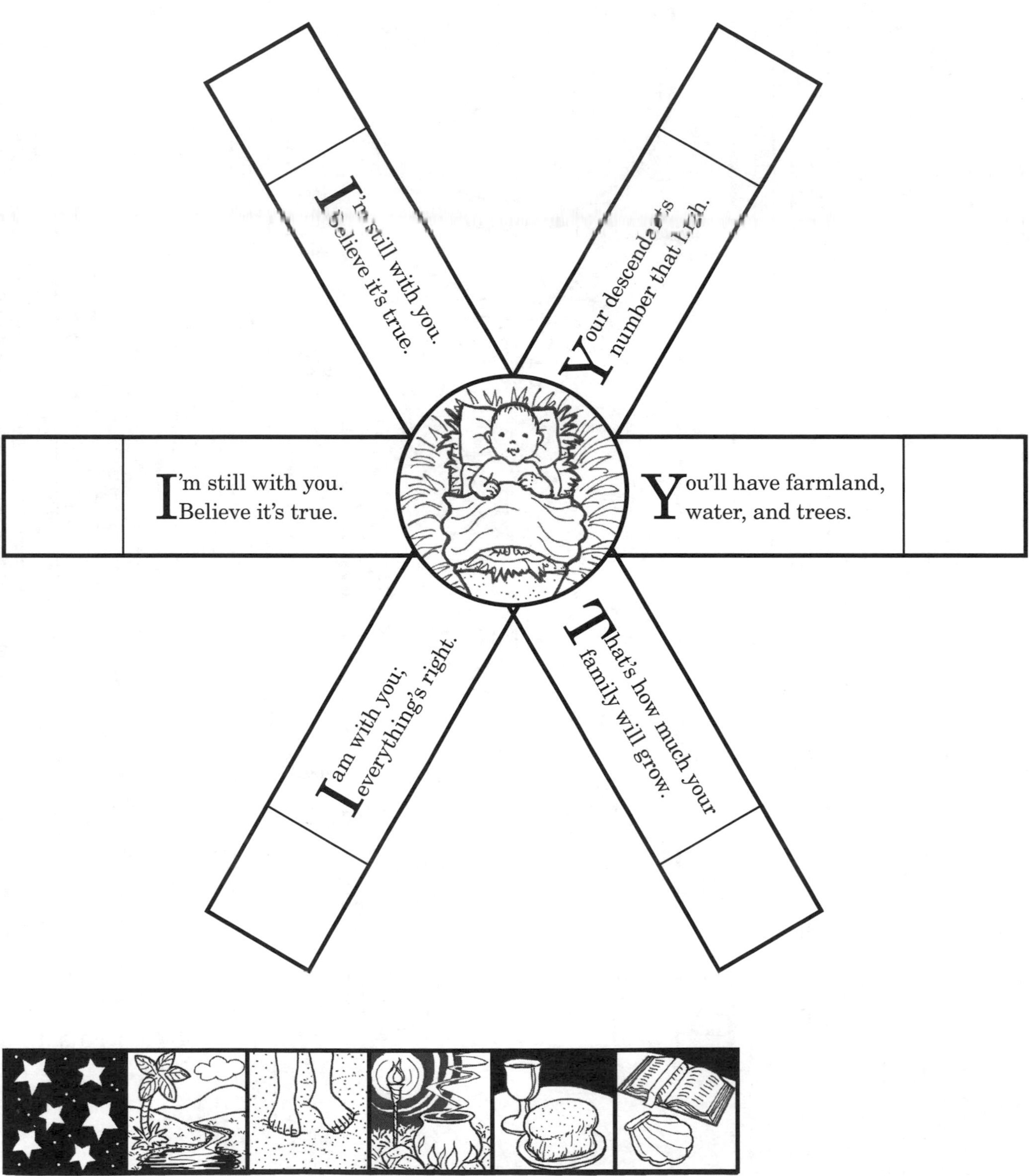
I'm still with you. Believe it's true.
Your descendants's number that Lich.
I'm still with you. Believe it's true.
You'll have farmland, water, and trees.
I am with you; everything's right.
That's how much your family will grow.

Ah, Lord God

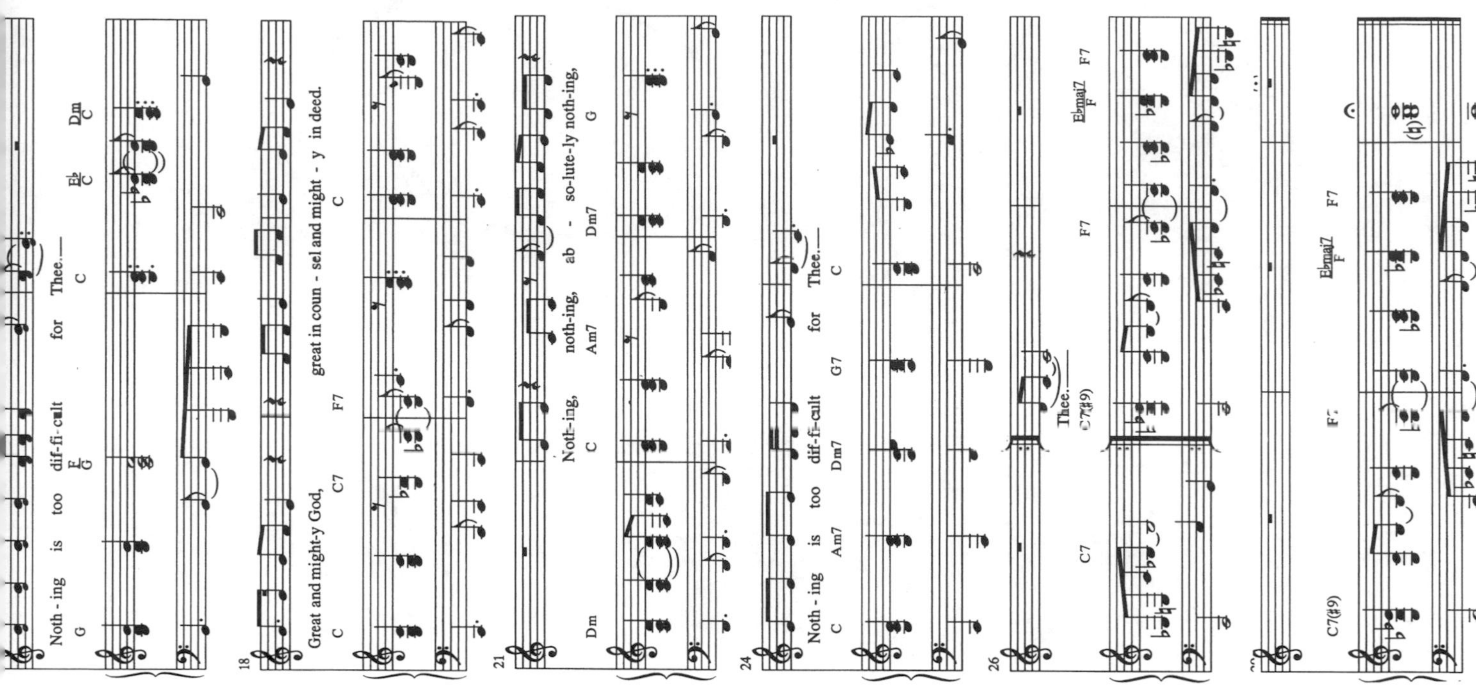

With a bluesy feel (♩=126)
Ah, Lord God, Thou hast made the heav-ens and the earth by Thy great pow-er;
Ah Lord God, Thou hast made the heav-ens and the earth by Thine out-stretched arm.
Noth-ing is too dif-fi-cult for Thee.
Noth-ing is too dif-fi-cult for Thee.
Great and might-y God, great in coun-sel and might-y in deed.
Noth-ing, noth-ing, ab-so-lute-ly noth-ing,
Noth-ing is too dif-fi-cult for Thee.
Thee.

God Turns My Heart Around

God
is
love.

Rocked By the Waves: Moses in His Basket

Bible Story:
The Birth of Moses (Exodus 2:1–10)

Materials:

Paper plate
Scissors
Marker
Sponge
Dish
Tempera paint (orange or brown)
Toy block
Fabric scraps
Glue
Blue yarn

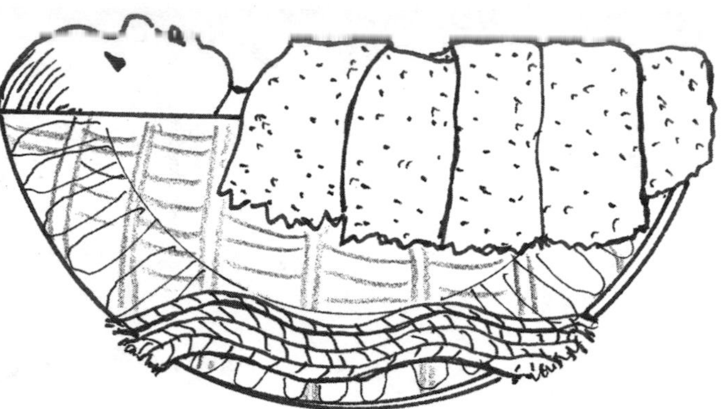

Directions:

1. Fold paper plate in half.
2. Draw a line 1½" below the folded edge of the plate for the top of the basket.
3. Using the illustration as a guide, outline Moses above the line you just drew, making sure that a part of the head and body touch the fold.
4. Cut the head and body as illustrated.
5. Draw in Moses' face.
6. Place the sponge in the dish. Pour a small amount of orange or brown tempera paint on the sponge.
7. Use the toy block to stamp paint over the outside of the paper plate. Let dry.
8. Cut fabric scraps and glue them on for Moses' blanket.
9. Cut pieces of blue yarn and glue them over the curved part of the basket for water.
10. Rock the plate back and forth. Pretend baby Moses is rocking in the river, waiting for Pharaoh's daughter to come and find him. Let the baby in the basket remind you that just as God took care of Moses long ago, He takes care of you today.

Suggestions:

1. Color the basket with crayons or markers.
2. Glue torn paper-bag pieces over the paper plate.
3. Use food coloring to dye macaroni pieces yellow and blue. Let dry and glue on for the basket and water.
4. Glue on vertical pieces of green yarn for bulrushes.

Unit 2

Words to Remember

9. Be obedient . . . show perfect courtesy toward all people. Titus 3:1–2

10. Behold, the Lamb of God, who takes away the sin of the world! John 1:29

11. When I am afraid, I will trust in You. Psalm 56:3 NIV

12. [God] provides you with plenty of food and fills your hearts with joy. Acts 14:17 NIV

13. You shall love the Lord your God with all your heart and with all your soul and with all your mind. Matthew 22:37

14. Be glad in the LORD, and rejoice. Psalm 32:11

15. Love surrounds the one who trusts in the LORD. Psalm 32:10

16. The LORD your God is with you wherever you go. Joshua 1:9

Dear Parents,

In the next few weeks, as we learn more about God's love, we will study how God blesses a nation. Your child will learn how the first families that they talked about in the last unit grew into a large nation. He or she will continue to see how God's children were His special, treasured possession. God delivered the Israelites from Pharaoh, provided for them in the wilderness and dwelt with them, and then led them to a new land.

Your child will be taught that God sees *us* as His treasured possession too. He delivers us from our enemies—sin, death, and the devil—through Jesus. He provides us with all that we need, and He is with us in His Word and Sacraments (Baptism and the Lord's Supper). He is preparing a new home for us in heaven, our promised land.

Again, read the Bible stories in *God Blesses a Nation* to your child. It's great to be God's loved people! Trust in God to take care of all your needs. Then praise God for being with us, guiding us, and blessing us—every day, everywhere!

Sharing the love of Jesus,
Your child's teacher

Assessment: Unit 2

Students can create a book to show how they recognize that God is with them and cares for them each day. They can make a "book-and-a-half" about themselves entitled "God Cares for Me" or "I Am Chosen by God." Take a full-body picture of each child; enlarge and print it twice, then glue each onto a 9 × 12-inch piece of construction paper. Use the full shot for the back cover, but cut off the top 4 inches (the head section), leaving the bottom 8 inches for the front cover. Staple this 9 × 8-inch cover and several 9 × 8-inch story pages (e.g., white construction paper) to the back cover with bottom edges even and the student's head visible at the top. On the pages, students draw their body doing things that show God's blessings (e.g., eating, reading, playing with or without friends, praying, reading the Bible, etc.). The student's face will stay the same, but as the pages are turned, a different image is shown. As they choose poses, students will need to consider how God is with them and cares for them every day and everywhere, just as He was with His people long ago. Note: If students can use digital cameras and pose in different settings, this could become a multimedia project, not just an art project.

Review the Unit 2 Word Wall Words. Encourage students to use as many as they can in journal writing.

Make a chart to compare being a member of the class, your church (congregation), and the whole Church body. Use the three headings: "classroom," "church," and "Church." Together as a class, fill in examples of how God has blessed each group in unique ways. Use two categories: "Saved us from ____" and "Gives us what we need:____."

At the end of the unit—and perhaps tying in with a social studies unit about communities and nations—give your students time to complete the following sentences and show their understanding of being a valued, responsible member of a group:

"Because I'm a ________ (list family last name), . . ."

"Because I'm in _______ (list your name)'s class, . . ."

"Because I'm an American, . . ."

"Because I'm God's child, . . ."

Your studies in this unit may provide a good opportunity to evaluate your classroom rules. Let each child list specific examples for each classroom rule, indicating his or her understanding of that concept. Give your class the opportunity to discuss (and perhaps even change) the rules, creating a list of suggestions called the First-Grade Amendments. After discussing the Ten Commandments, the students might also like to add new rules to the existing class list.

Show an American flag. Ask your students to write a few thoughts about "What the American flag Means to Me." Show a Christian flag. Ask your students to write a few thoughts about "What the Christian Flag Means to Me." Do any of your students have a family crest? Ask if they can explain the design. If they don't have a family crest, encourage them to design one.

Think *in*side the box. One at a time, take a picture of each of your students inside a box. Pretend that the box is a treasure chest, or decorate it to look like one. Drape necklaces around the students' necks and let them hold coins or jewels. Display the pictures in the hallway. Beneath each picture, post that student's response when asked to complete one of the following sentences: "I know God treasures me because . . ." or "I'm God's treasured possession because . . ."

Do a "Law and Gospel" activity. Give your students time to think about the following:

1. Who are my enemies?
2. Why I don't like sin
3. Why I don't like the devil

Follow up with a prayer, full of the reassurance that we are saved from sin, death, and the devil because Jesus died on the cross and rose again to bring us life. "Thank You, God, for saving me from my enemies, sin, death, and the devil. In Jesus' name I pray. Amen."

Give students a blank bulleted or numbered list. Together as a class or individually, create a how-to list or book: "How to Worship the Lord with Gladness."

Create individual "My Book About Heaven" mini books. Give students time to draw pictures and write a sentence for each page. Suggestions for page topics include: "What I think heaven will look like," "Whom I will see in heaven," "What we will do in heaven," "What I think the angels do in heaven," and "Why I think they call heaven 'the promised land.'"

Have each student pretend that he or she is a child in the Israelite nation who is friends with an Egyptian child who had become a follower of God while the Israelites were living in Egypt. What if they could correspond with each other? Help students create a class envelope book filled with letters to Egyptian children from each of your students. Cut the flap off envelopes (all the same size). Allow each child to develop his or her own Egyptian pen pal's name and address (e.g., Thutmose, 123 Pyramid Way, Egypt) to address the envelope. (Use the Internet to look up name possibilities, if desired.) Students can design their own stamp. Give each student paper to write a letter to their Egyptian friend, talking about life since they left Egypt (e.g., the Exodus, manna, the Ten Commandments, and the tent church). To form a book, place several envelopes between two cover sheets. Bind or staple the left side and write the title "Letters from the Wilderness" on the front cover.

For critical thinking, ask an open-ended question like "What do we praise God for?" Allow students to respond by journaling or speaking their answer.

Make a bulletin board for the song "Kids of the Kingdom" (*SKLS2*, pp. 38–39). Show a picture of each student. Below the picture, write the following heading and each child's response: "My name is ____ I love the Lord." Have them write at least one sentence about why they love the Lord and post it under their picture.

Use Web Resource Unit2a to review where the Children of Israel have been and where they are going in a visual and hands-on way.

MATH
Coach

Behold, the
Lamb of God,
who takes
away the sin
of the world!

John 1:29

God SAVED His people from Pharaoh.

God SAVED us from sin through Jesus.

They COMPLAINED instead of being thankful for God's care.

We COMPLAIN instead of being thankful for God's gifts.

God GAVE bread and meat.

God GIVES us daily bread and things like __________.

God CARED for His people. He promised a Savior to meet their biggest need.

God CARES for us. He meets our biggest need through Jesus, feeding us through His Word and the Lord's Supper.

confess
1
2
3
4
5
6
7
8
9
10

God makes me His child.
God forgives my sin.
God tells me about Jesus.
I can sing.
I can pray.
I can give.

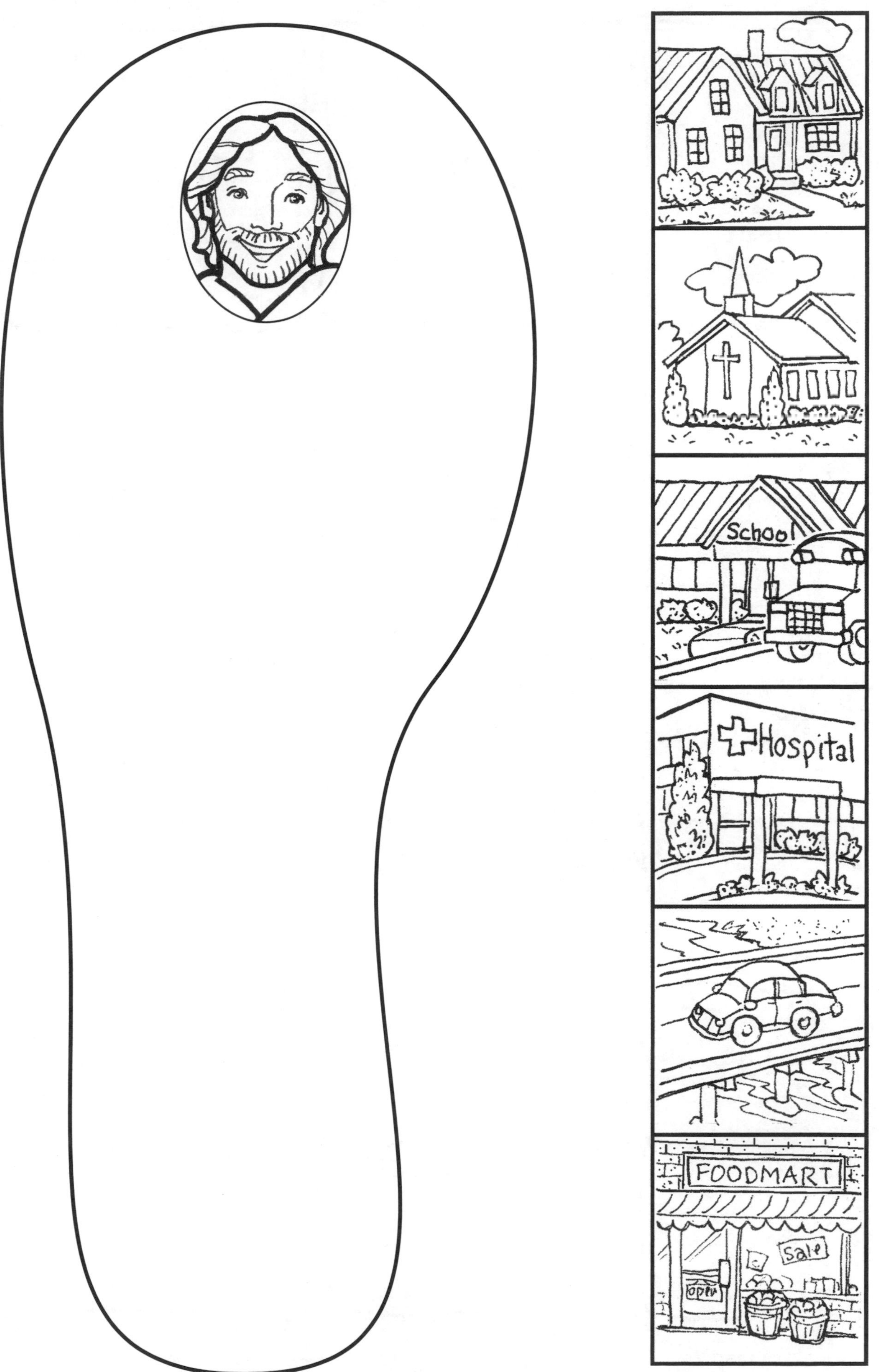
School
Hospital
FOODMART
Sale
open

The	Lord	your
God	is	with
you	wherever	you
go.	Joshua	1:9

Unit 3

Words to Remember

17. It is the LORD who goes before you. He will be with you. . . . Do not fear. Deuteronomy 31:8

18. Be strong in the LORD and in the strength of His might. Ephesians 6:10

19. The LORD is near to all who call on Him. Psalm 145:18

20. [Jesus said,] "I chose you and appointed you that you should go and bear fruit." John 15:16

21. The LORD is my rock and my fortress and my deliverer . . . my shield, and the horn of my salvation. Psalm 18:2

22. Oh come, let us worship and bow down; let us kneel before the LORD, our Maker! Psalm 95:6

23. Give thanks to the LORD, for His steadfast love endures forever. 2 Chronicles 20:21

24. Be strong and courageous. Do not be frightened . . . for the LORD your God is with you wherever you go. Joshua 1:9

Dear Parents,

In the next few weeks, as we learn more about God's love, we will study how God blesses leaders. Your child will see that God works through leaders to bless His people. These leaders were just ordinary humans, but through God's power and His grace, amazing things happened. Your child will study Deborah, Samson, Samuel, David, Solomon, Jehoshaphat, and Esther.

Through these stories, your child will see how God provided for His people and guided them. But most importantly, your child will see how God, through Jesus, saved them from their enemies of sin, death, and the devil. And He does the same for us! The most important and effective aspect of these leaders' lives was their reliance on God. In their lives and in ours today, the true leader, the great hero, is God Himself.

Just as God equipped these leaders, He also equips your child to be a leader who relies on God, follows God's will, and blesses others with his or her gifts. May God also bless you in the same way in your leadership role in your family. Together with your child, pray for leaders in sports, government, entertainment, or whatever field, that they may rely on Jesus as they speak, act, and make their decisions.

Sharing the love of Jesus,
Your child's teacher

Assessment: **Unit 3**

Tie your study of leaders into Election Day. Ask students, **Although we know that God appointed these leaders we've been studying, if you lived in Bible times why would you vote for (Deborah, Samson, David, etc.) as (judge, king, etc.)?** What qualities or character traits made them or would make them good leaders? Brainstorm words (e.g., *brave, strong, trusting*) on the board. To remind students that God called these leaders, you may want to look at voting posters and create a template for your students to fill in these attributes. For example, include room for a picture of the leader and a phrase or two such as "Vote for me because "I am ______," or "I believe in ______," or "I stand for _______," or "_______is what's important to me," or "I will _______ for you."

At the completion of the unit, encourage your students to choose a favorite leader from those studied in Unit 3 (Deborah, Samson, Samuel, David, Solomon, Jehoshaphat, Esther). Allow them to choose their favorite form of communication to share why they chose that person. They could dress up like the leader and give a monologue. They could draw or paint a portrait of the leader and write a few sentences to post below the picture.

Tie the unit in with your study of Martin Luther and the Reformation. Use the CPH product *The Story of Martin Luther*. At the end of your studies, can your students fill in the following blanks? "Martin Luther stood up for God when he ___________." "Deborah [Esther] stood up for God when she _________." "Samson [David or Jehoshaphat] stood up for God when he ________."

Throughout the month, pass out award ribbons each day to the students who exhibit the same character qualities as the leaders that you are or will be studying. Students will begin to associate the Old Testament leaders with these traits without study and drill. Recognize students for displaying the following qualities: peace-making (demonstrating the ability to mediate and resolve conflicts) like Deborah, strength like Samson, eagerness and willingness like Samuel, a heart for the Lord like David, wisdom like Solomon, trust or a thankful heart like Jehoshaphat, and courage/bravery like Esther. Be sure to give every student an award; because some children may not be as likely to draw attention to themselves, you may have to make a special effort to make note of their behavior. At your brief "award ceremony" each day, remember to close with a prayer thanking God for making us able (enabling us) to bless others with these attributes. It is **He** who gives us these gifts.

Review the Unit 3 Word Wall Words. Encourage students to use as many as they can in journal writing.

Play a Guess Who-type game or Twenty Questions, where you give clues about a leader's identity. Students may only ask yes or no questions to limit their search. Can students guess the character in three questions? in ten? in twenty?

After the unit, have students complete the following two sentences, "I am most like _________." "I want to be like ________." Students can list at least two reasons why the felt they are like Esther, David, and so on.

Read off the following quotes; have students decide who's talking. List the characters on the board (e.g., 1. Deborah, 2. Samson, 3. Samuel, 4. David, 5. Solomon, 6. Jehoshaphat, 7. Esther). Students could indicate their choice by writing the number of the correct leader on their paper or by holding up the correct number of fingers on their hand (although in order to keep the results private, you may want the students to put their head down on their desk, resting their wrists at the top of their desk).

"What shall be done for the man who kills this Philistine and takes away the reproach from Israel? For who is this . . . Philistine, that he should defy the armies of the living God?" (David to Israelite army, 1 Samuel 17:26)

"Let me now put a riddle to you." (Samson to the Philistines, Judges 14:12)

"O LORD, God of our fathers, are You not God in heaven? You rule over all the kingdoms of the nations. In Your hand are power and might, so that none is able to withstand You. . . . We are powerless against this great horde that is coming against us. We do not know what to do, but our eyes are on You." (Jehoshaphat to people of Judah, 2 Chronicles 20:6–12)

"Up! For this is the day in which the LORD has given Sisera into your hand. Does not the LORD go out before you?" (Deborah to Barak, Judges 4:13-14)

"The LORD has not chosen these. . . . Are all your sons here?" (Samuel to Jesse, 1 Samuel 16:10)

"If my head is shaved, my strength will leave me, and I shall become weak and be like any other man." (Samson to Delilah, Judges 16:17)

"I intend to build a house for the name of the LORD my God, as the LORD said to David my father, 'Your son, whom I will set on your throne in your place, shall build the house for My name.'" (Solomon to Hiram, the king of Tyre, 1 Kings 5:5)

"If I have found favor in your sight, O king, and if it please the king, let my life be granted me for my wish, and my people for my request. For we have been sold, I and my people, to be destroyed, to be killed." (Esther to King Ahasuerus, Esther 7:3–4)

"The LORD who delivered me from the paw of the lion and from the paw of the bear will deliver me from the hand of this Philistine." (David to King Saul, 1 Samuel 17:37)

"O LORD, God of Israel, there is no God like You, in heaven above or on earth beneath, keeping covenant and showing steadfast love to Your servants who walk before You with all their heart, who have kept with Your servant David my father what You declared to him." (Solomon at temple dedication, 1 Kings 8:23–24)

"You come to me with a sword and with a spear and with a javelin, but I come to you in the name of the LORD of hosts, the God of the armies of Israel, whom you have defied." (David to Goliath, 1 Samuel 17:45)

Use Web Resource Unit 3a to have students engage their visual learning skills in review of the stories. Slowly reveal the Bible characters from this unit, using the tool that comes with your software. Begin by revealing only a small section that shows an object in the picture that might give a clue about the character from the context (e.g., an angel on the ark of the covenant), then enlarge the area little by little (e.g., show the whole ark of the covenant and then the temple), and finally start to reveal the person's face. Can your students guess the character before you reveal the entire image?

Throughout the unit, be sure to pray for current leaders in your school, church, community, state, and nation. Pray that they put their trust in God and follow His will. At the end of the unit, you may want students to write their own prayer for leaders, which might show their understanding.

Lead us not into temptation.

Prayer List

We trust in God's promise to give us what we need, including God-fearing leaders. Draw lines to match the words and the leaders God gives us. You will notice that two pictures are missing. After matching all the pictures, see what is left. Find out what to draw and then complete the activity.

Directions

1. Color the person to look like you.
2. Cut out the person.
3. Cut out the little circle inside the heart.
4. Cut out the big circle and place stickers on the little circles.
5. Attach the big circle to the back of body using a brad.

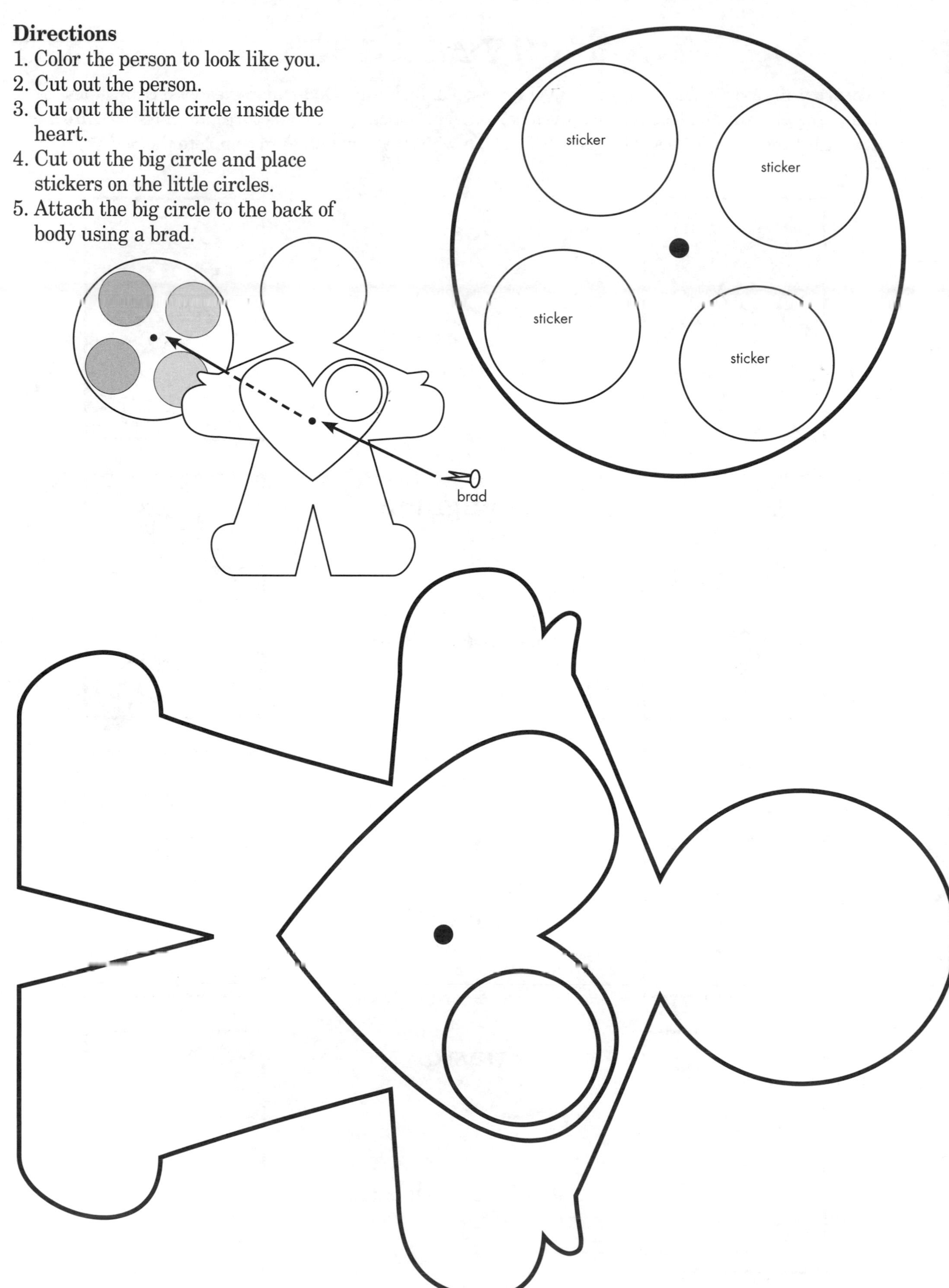

Directions

1. Cut along the solid line.
2. Color the horn.
3. Add glue along one side with small stars, bring it under the other edge with stars, and carefully roll the paper into a cone.
4. Press together the glued edges until they are secure.

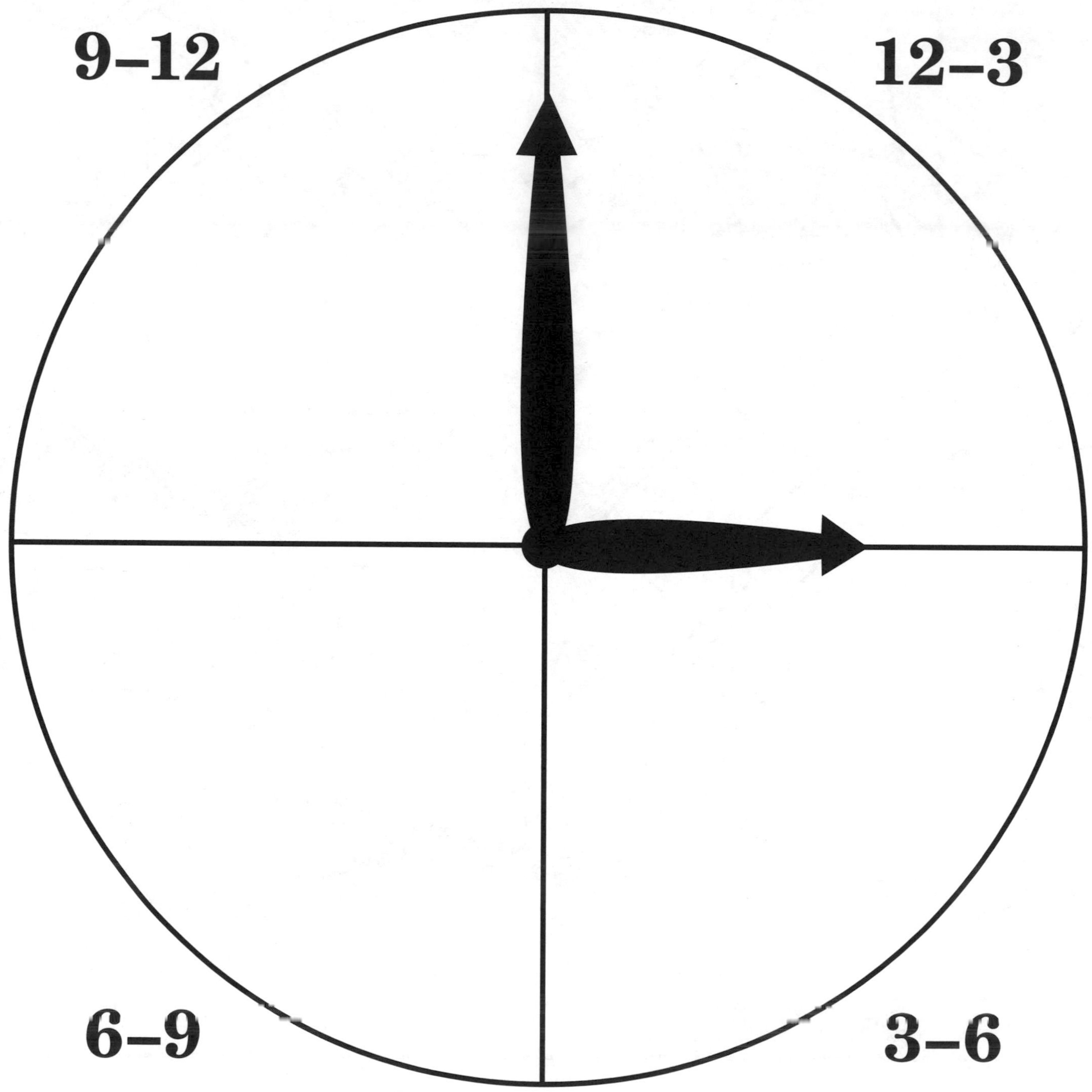

Time is a gift from God. We can use it to His glory.

Think about an average Sunday in your family. What do you do at certain times of day? Draw a picture or write down the types of activities you do during these times.

God's
LOVE
never
ends.

God Helps Us Do What Is Right

God says, "You shall have no other gods."

God says, "You shall not steal."

God says, "Remember the Sabbath day by keeping it holy."

God says, "You shall not give false testimony against your neighbor."

God says, "Honor your father and your mother."

God says, "You shall not covet."

Unit 4

Words to Remember

25. Sing to Him, sing praise to Him; tell of all His wonderful acts. Psalm 105:2 NIV

26. I am with you always, to the end of the age. Matthew 28:20

27. Trust in the LORD with all your heart. Proverbs 3:5

28. Go therefore and make disciples of all nations, baptizing them in the name of the Father and of the Son and of the Holy Spirit. Matthew 28:19

29. Fear not, for I am with you. Isaiah 43:5

30. For [God] will command His angels concerning you to guard you in all your ways. Psalm 91:11

31. Repent, then, and turn to God, so that your sins may be wiped out. Acts 3:19 NIV

32. For to us a child is born, to us a son is given. Isaiah 9:6

Dear Parents,

In the next few weeks, as we learn more about God's love, we will study how God uses others to share His Word. Your child will learn how the Old Testament prophets reminded people of their sin and their need to change their behavior (the Law), but also how the prophets shared God's forgiveness and grace (the Gospel) with His people.

When your child hears the prophets' words of comfort, hope, forgiveness, and life, he or she will be reassured themselves, and then will be encouraged to share that Good News with others. The Holy Spirit strengthens your child's faith and gives your child confidence to tell others that God is with us, that God listens to our prayers, and that God forgives our sins and gives us a new life through Jesus.

Again, read the Bible stories in *God Speaks through Prophets* to your child. God can speak through you too! Share your own convictions with your child, sharing how you've been assured that God is with you, hears your prayers, and forgives your wrongs. Look for times your child may share words of God's love and forgiveness with others and praise him or her for the courage to do so. Every day, you and your child can point each other to Jesus.

Sharing the love of Jesus,
Your child's teacher

Assessment: Unit 4

At the end of the unit, review story facts with riddle bags. Put a picture of each prophet (e.g., Elijah, Elisha, Jonah, Isaiah, Daniel) in a separate brown bag. On the outside of the bag, write three clues about each character (e.g., was not liked by King Ahab, challenged the prophets of Baal to a contest, prayed that God would send fire to the altar he built). Can students select/recognize the correct prophet before peeking inside the bag for the answer? Test individually to most specifically track comprehension and retention, even recording whether students guess the character with one, two, or three clues. You may choose to reveal only one clue at a time. To test the class's comprehension, in general, review as a whole-class activity. To challenge students, have them work in threesomes or small groups to develop their own clues. Provide only the bag containing a prophet's picture.

At the end of the unit, hold a sensory test. Provide something from each story that students can touch, taste, see, smell, or hear that will remind them of a certain Bible story from the unit. Some possibilities include a campfire-scented candle (Elijah and the Prophets of Baal); a wheel from a toy car or even a chair (Elijah Goes to Heaven); a can of tuna, sardines, or crabmeat (Jonah); an empty pill or medicine bottle (Hezekiah's Prayer); something sharp, yet safe such as a toothpick, shark's tooth, or fake fangs and/or faux fur (Daniel in the Lions' Den); pretend silver and gold coins (God's People Return Home); a pacifier or baby bottle to represent a baby's birth, even though Jesus wouldn't have used either one (Prophets Tell of the Savior). You may want to blindfold students when they use their sense of touch or smell.

Review the Unit 4 Word Wall Words. Encourage students to use as many as they can in journal writing.

Life application skills are often assessed by observation. Create a "religion clipboard." Put index cards or sticky notes on the clipboard with the following questions (one question per card): "Are they sharing Jesus with others?" "Do they know God is with them?" "Do they know God answers prayers?" "Do they know God is the one true God?" "Do they know God forgives?" "Do they show sorrow for their sinful actions?" When you observe a child showing comprehension through their words or actions, write their name and the date on the appropriate card. Encourage parents also to look for evidence of these things and share with you (e.g., suggested the family prays for someone, asked for forgiveness of a sin without prompting, mentioned Jesus in a conversation outside of religion class or a family devotion).

Make a chart with three to five columns. At the top of each column, write the following headings: consequences, comfort, hope, forgiveness, life. Work together as a class to develop at least one or two examples of a phrase that could be spoken to represent that concept. To prompt students, provide a context (e.g., someone's dog died, someone called another child a name, someone didn't wear his coat outside) and have children decide what phrase could be said. To make it easier, provide students with a phrase (e.g., "Jesus is with you," "I forgive you," "Uh-oh. You're gonna [get a ticket, move to red—whatever your classroom consequence is]"), and let them categorize what was said according to one of the headings.

At the end of the unit, see if students remember their facts with a fill-in-the-blank activity. Provide the following words in a word box on your board: Elijah, Jonah, Daniel, People of Nineveh, Jesus, Elisha, Shunammite woman, King Darius. Use the following sentences:

1. I was amazed that the lions did not harm Daniel. (King Darius)
2. I was taken up to heaven in a whirlwind. (Elijah)
3. We had turned away from God and needed to repent. (People of Nineveh)
4. The prophets were all telling the people about putting their trust in Me. (Jesus)
5. I was a rich woman who was lonely and always wanted a child. (Shunammite woman)
6. I tried to run away and hide from God. (Jonah)
7. I refused to obey the rules of the king. (Daniel)
8. I told a woman of God's promise of new life and the hope we have in God's Word. (Elisha)

At the end of the unit, see if students can match the following settings and main characters:

The prophet Ezra—traveling to the temple in Jerusalem

The prophet Micah— mentioned Bethlehem as the town in which the Savior would be born

The prophet Daniel—living in Babylon, Nebuchadnezzar's kingdom

King Hezekiah—ruling in the Israelites' land (kingdom of Judah)

The prophet Jonah—traveling in a boat on the Mediterranean Sea; also preaching in Nineveh

The prophet Elisha—staying at a Shunammite woman's house

The prophet Elijah—crossed over the Jordan River

At the end of each story, discuss as a class: How did the prophet show he had confidence? What did he confess? Say a prayer that the Holy Spirit makes the students confident and gives them the right words to say or the right actions to do, at the right time.

You may want to use the bulletin board idea as an assessment, either at the end of the unit or as you complete each story. Create your own worksheet by writing the following phrases inside a speech bubble and having students draw lines to match the character with what they learned.

"God is the one true God." (Elijah) "God is with me." (Elisha) "God's Word brings life." (Shunammite woman) "God forgives us." (Ninevites) "God listens to my prayers." (King Hezekiah) "God is the most powerful king." (Daniel and King Nebuchadnezzar) "God's Word helps us rebuild our lives." (Ezra) "God will send a Savior." (Isaiah)

Go see Ahab.

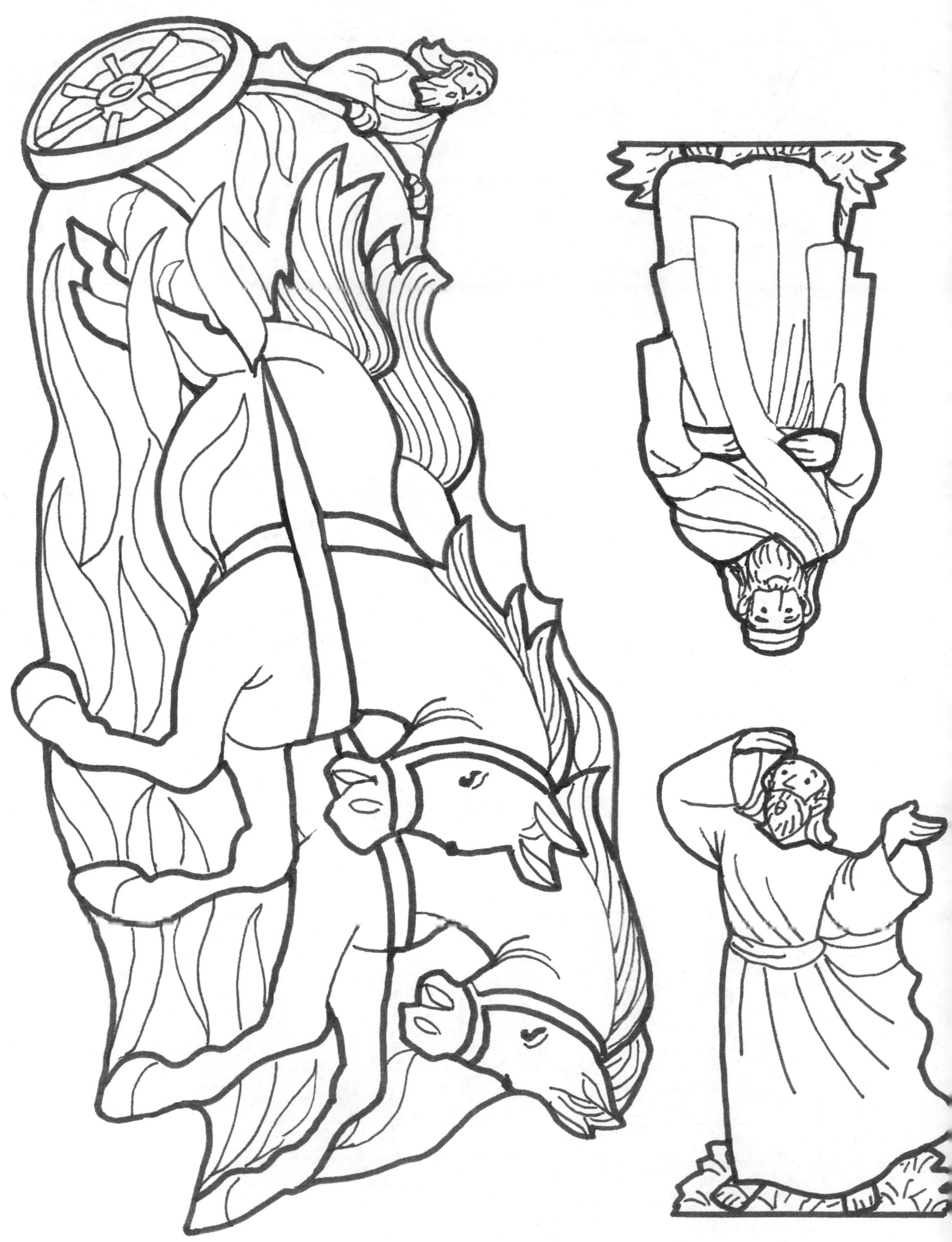

Trust in the LORD with all your heart.

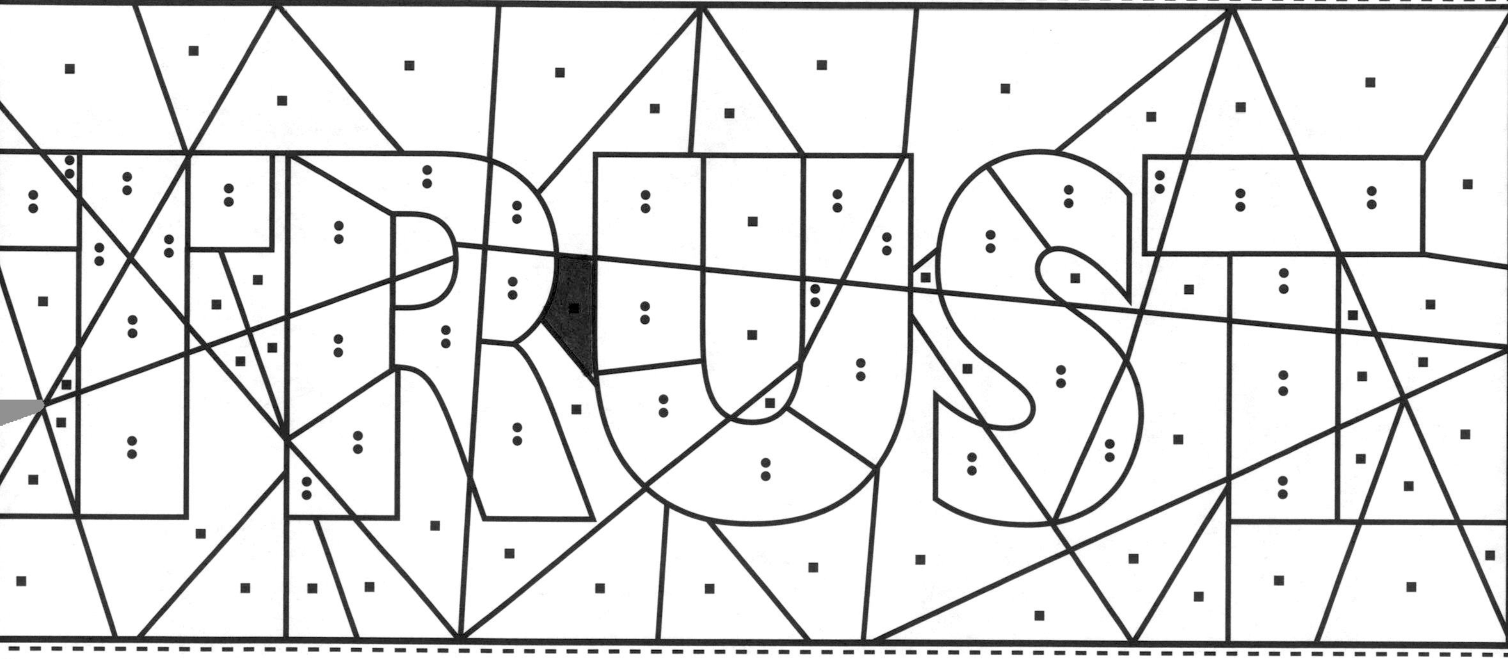

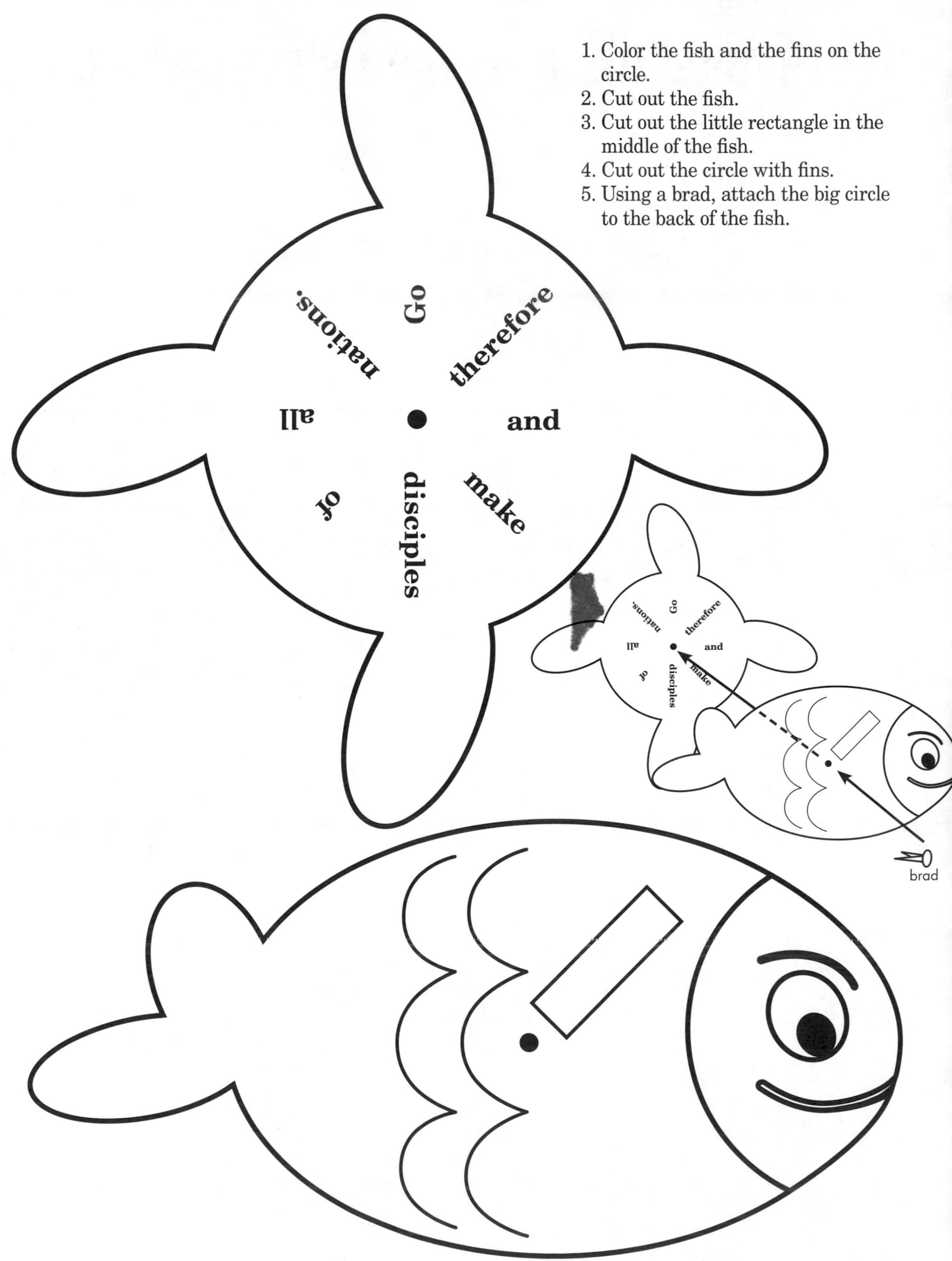
1. Color the fish and the fins on the circle.
2. Cut out the fish.
3. Cut out the little rectangle in the middle of the fish.
4. Cut out the circle with fins.
5. Using a brad, attach the big circle to the back of the fish.
Go
therefore
and
make
disciples
of
all
nations.
brad

No Fear!

Dear

Lord

Save

Me

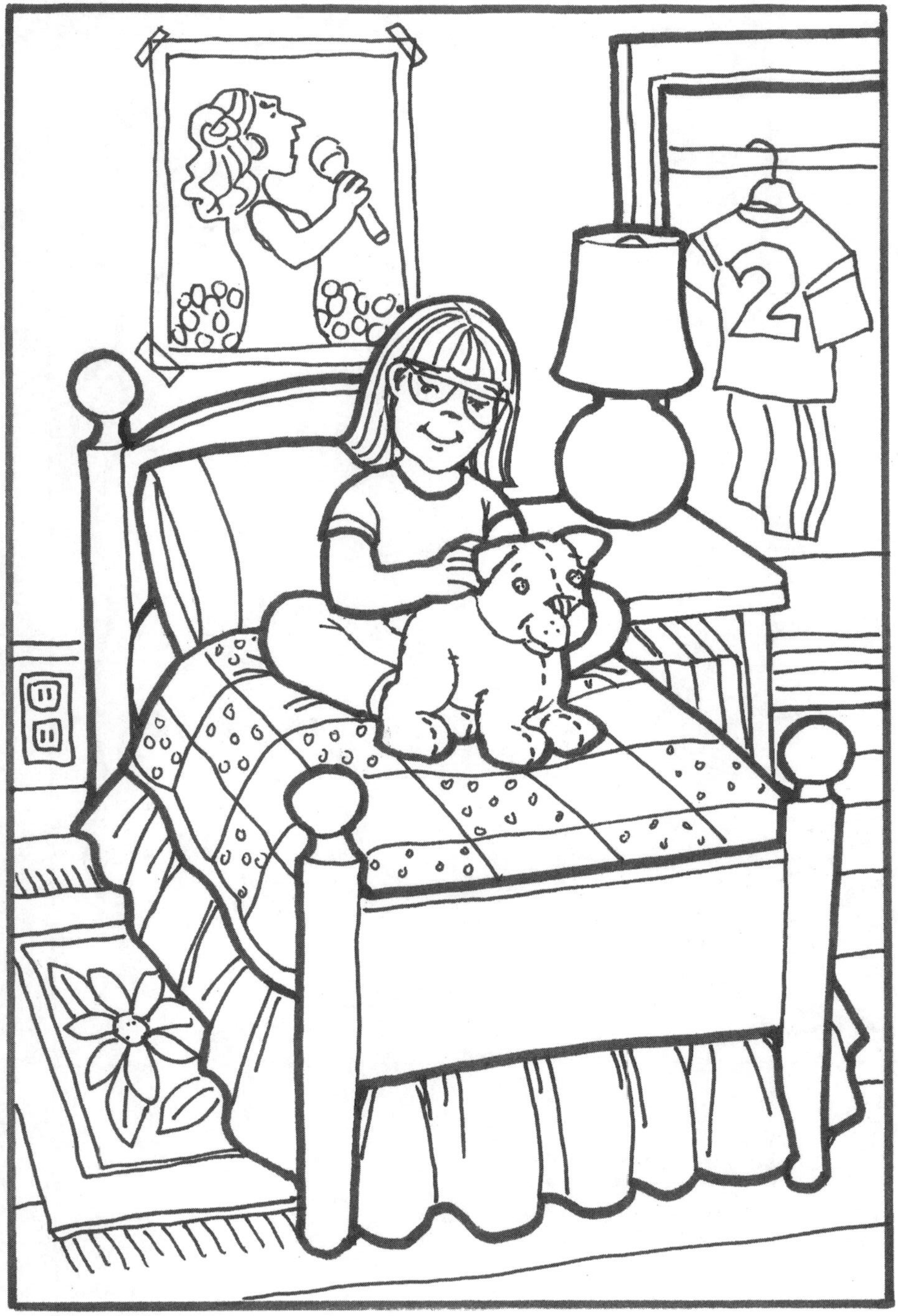

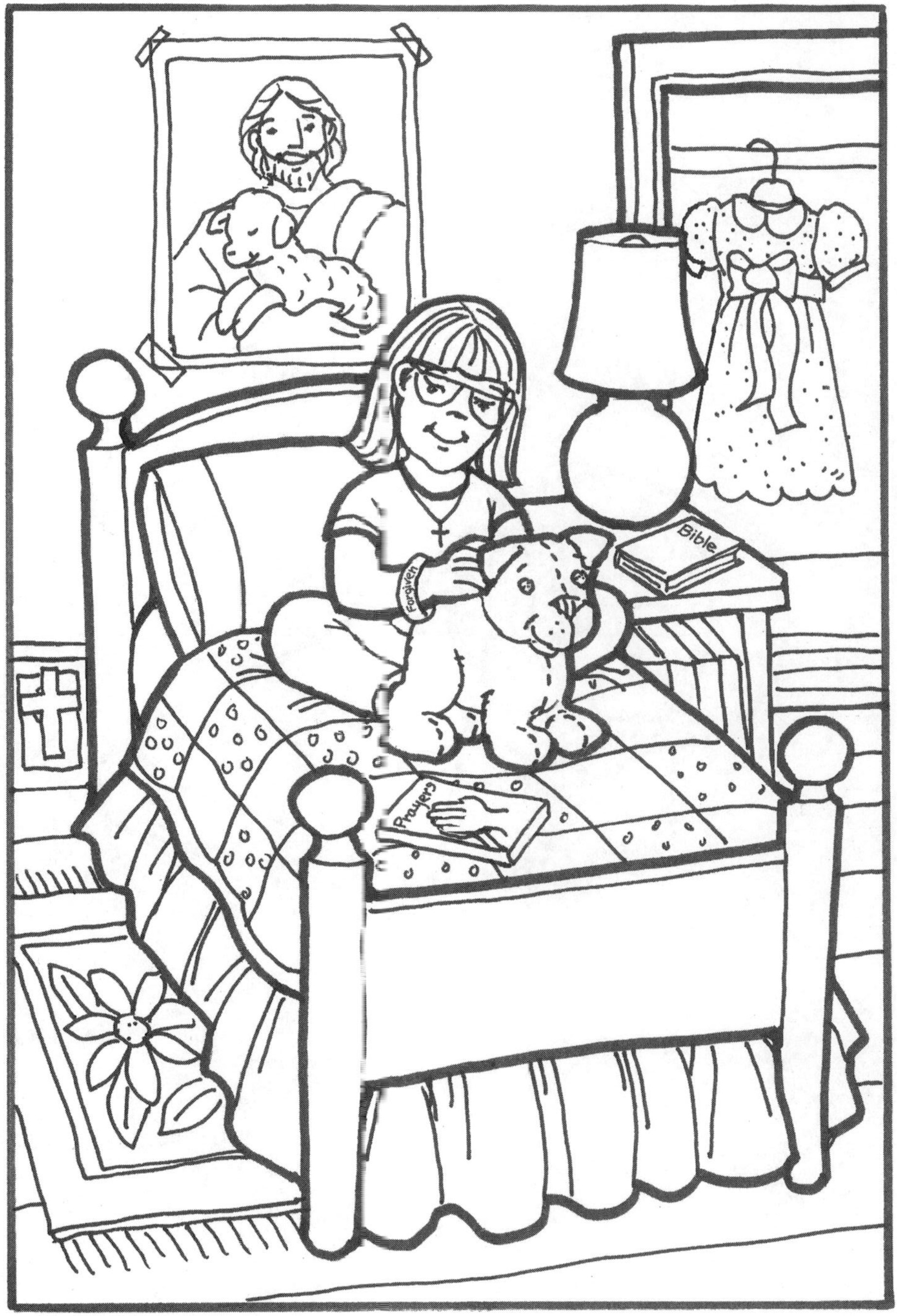
Bible
Forgiven
Prayers

1. Cut around edge.
2. Color.
3. Cut on dotted lines.
4. Fold down. Flip.
5. Draw baby Jesus.

Unit 5

Words to Remember

33. For nothing will be impossible with God. Matthew 1:37

34. "For unto you is born this day in the city of David a Savior, who is Christ the Lord." Luke 2:11

35. The grace of God has appeared, bringing salvation for all people. Titus 2:11

36. You are all sons of God through faith in Christ Jesus, for all of you who were baptized into Christ have clothed yourselves with Christ. Galatians 3:26–27 (NIV)

37. My sheep hear My voice, and I know them, and they follow Me. John 10:27

38. For God so loved the world, that He gave His only Son, that whoever believes in Him should not perish but have eternal life. John 3:16

39. [God] has sent Me to proclaim liberty to the captives. Luke 4:18

40. [Jesus said] "Let the children come to Me; do not hinder them, for to such belongs the kingdom of God." Mark 10:14

Dear Parents,

In the next few weeks, as we learn more about God's love, we will study the coming of the Savior. Your child will learn *how* God sent His Son as he or she studies the stories of the angel visiting Mary and Christmas. As he or she studies the stories of Christmas, Jesus' Baptism, and Nicodemus, your child will learn *why* God sent His Son, our Savior: because of His great love for His children, so that we would receive forgiveness and salvation. Your child will learn that the Savior came for all people as he or she studies the stories of Simeon and Anna, Nicodemus, Jesus preaching, and Jesus blessing the children. As he or she studies the stories of Jesus calling His disciples and Jesus preaching, your child will learn how we hear and receive this Good News of our Savior through God's Word.

The story of our Savior, God's only Son, coming down to earth for the purpose of saving us from our sins gives us Christmas joy throughout the year. Your child will know that Jesus would do this just for him or her, because he or she is that special to God. One of the songs your child will learn summarizes it well: "Someone Special, who would give His own Son that all might live, And by Him would set us free From all sin and misery. Someone special I must be, Since You gave Your Son for me!" (*All God's People Sing!*, p. 217).

Read the Bible stories in "The Savior Comes" to your child. Reassure your child of your own love for him or her as you spend time together, share compliments, praise him or her for specific tasks well done, and simply enjoy being together. The forgiveness and unconditional love your child receives from you will speak volumes about your own love, and it models our heavenly Father's love. Remember that you are God's beloved child too. Our heavenly Father cares about you and your challenges; He cared enough to send a Savior so that you would live together as a family forever in heaven.

Sharing the love of Jesus,
Your child's teacher

Assessment: Unit 5

Play a game called What's Wrong with the Story? Review story facts by creating silly, nonsensical stories and having children edit them by crossing out a word (or words) and writing the correct word(s) above it (them). Provide a word bank if necessary. Here are some examples for starters, but you will probably want to include more. Only change what you expect students to remember, not obscure information (e.g., people, numbers, locations, etc.).

"The Angel Visits Mary": Mary was visited by the angel *Gabriella*. (Gabriel) Mary did *not* believe the angel. (Cross out "not").

"Jesus, Our Savior, Is Born": Mary and Joseph traveled to *Bermuda*. (Bethlehem) It was crowded in town because of the *football game*. (census) They had to sleep in the *penthouse suite*. (stable, barn)

"Simeon and Anna": The *president* told Simeon that this baby was the Savior. (Holy Spirit) When Simeon saw Jesus, he *did a jig*. (held the baby in his arms)

"The Baptism of Jesus": When John saw Jesus, he said, *"What up, cuz?"* ("I need to be baptized by You, not You be baptized by me"; or "Behold, the Lamb of God!") When Jesus went up from the water, a *crow* came down to rest on Jesus. (dove)

"Jesus Calls His Disciples": When Andrew learned that Jesus was the Messiah, he ran to tell his brother *William*. (Simon Peter) Jesus told Nathanael that He saw him under the *Christmas tree*. (fig tree)

"Nicodemus Visits Jesus": Nicodemus met Jesus *in a crowded mall*. (secretly, alone, at night) Jesus said we must be born again by water and *soap*. (the Holy Spirit)

"Jesus Preaches at Nazareth": Jesus did *many* miracles for them. (Change "many" to "no" or add the words "did not do.") The people of Nazareth wanted to throw Jesus off *the roof.* (a cliff)

"Jesus Blesses the Children": The parents brought their children to Jesus so He could *play games with them*. (bless them) *The Pharisees* told the parents to leave Jesus alone. (The disciples)

Review the Unit 5 Word Wall Words. Encourage students to use as many as they can in journal writing.

Mary sang a song. The angels sang a song. Simeon sang a song. Can your students? Allow students to work together in groups or as the whole class to write a stanza for a song sung to the tune of "Joy to the World." Write the following rhyming words on the board, or brainstorm others: *king*, *sing*, *ring*, *bring*, *offering*, *cling*, *spring*, *sting*, *swing*, *thing*, *wing*, *something*, *everything*.

Ask the children to respond to this question: "What did they do when they saw the Savior, Jesus?" Students can provide an answer for each of the following persons or groups: the shepherds, Simeon and Anna, John the Baptist, and Andrew and the other disciples. You might also include the people of Nazareth and the little children. Give students the option of answering in whatever form they prefer (e.g., acting it out or pantomiming the response; drawing a picture for each response; writing a sentence or two for each response; even singing about what happened). For a more personal question, have them answer, "What do *you* do when you see Jesus, our Savior, in God's Word, in Baptism, and in the Lord's Supper?" Can they recall a time when they responded in praise?

God loved us so much that He sent His one and only Son to be our Savior. Jesus loved us so much that He did His Father's will, coming down from heaven to earth to suffer and die to be our Savior. Just as Jesus showed compassion to the children He blessed, He shows all of His children how much He cares. In response, have students write a prayer about showing compassion and love to others *themselves*. Does their prayer reflect a desire to show others that they are important in God's eyes or a desire to share Jesus' love with all people? To daily remind them of Jesus' love and of their call to live a Spirit-filled life, following God's ways, provide fabric markers for students to write their prayer on their own pillowcase. (You may want to first slide a piece of cardboard inside the pillowcase so the marker won't bleed through and so students have a flat surface to write on.) Each night, they can pray that they will reflect Jesus' love and compassion.

After the story of Jesus' Baptism, play a substitute game. Go around the circle and give each student a chance to participate. Provide the context (typically a noun, but it could be a verb): "Instead of __________" (e.g., using butter, using a crayon, using a pencil, choosing vanilla)." Let students contribute an alternate idea: "you can __________" (e.g., use margarine, use a marker, use a pencil, choose chocolate). End the game by reviewing how Jesus was our Substitute and took the punishment for our sins, in our place. Jesus carried our sins so we don't have to.

Read the book *Christmas Around the World* by Brenda Trunkhill (available from CPH). Have students write prayers for those in other countries who may not yet know about our Savior and/or for those in other countries who are trying to tell others about our Savior. You may even want to look up the names of specific missionaries in those regions and pray that God would bless their efforts. Pray a different child's prayer each morning at your classroom devotion time, and/or make a class prayer book to send home. To visually represent the prayer that everyone around the world will know the Good News about their Savior, the prayers could even be written on a roll of adding machine paper and wrapped around a globe or a picture of the earth.

After the story of Simeon and Anna or Jesus Blesses the Children, have students consider: "Do I treat people differently?" "Is there anyone I can be nicer to?" Help each child make his or her own New Year's resolutions by filling in an empty January calendar. Students can write or draw one goal (e.g., "Be nice to my sister," "Put away my toys," "Do my homework without complaining," "Open the door for others," etc.) for each day.

Have students consider the question "What if our Savior, Jesus, never came?" Students could write individual responses, or you may want to use this as a think, pair, share activity. Discuss as a class: "Why were people waiting for Jesus?" Share with students that some people actually still *are* waiting for the Savior to come. Learn about The Apple of His Eye Mission Society at Web Resource Unit 5a.

Words to Remember
“____ ________ ____ __ __________ _____ _____.”
Luke 1:37

Dear ____________________,

Merry Christmas! Jesus is born! Come and celebrate His birth with my family. We invite you to worship with us on December ____, ____________.

Our Christmas worship begins at ____________________.

We'd love to share our Christmas with you!

In Jesus' Love,

Our Church's Address:

____

____

____

(__________)____________________

____

For unto you is born this day in the city of David a Savior, who is Christ the Lord.

Luke 2:11

The grace of God has appeared, bringing salvation for all people.

Titus 2:11

I'm in God's family.
I have peace with God.
I'm forgiven.
I am God's child.

Jesus loves me and calls me.

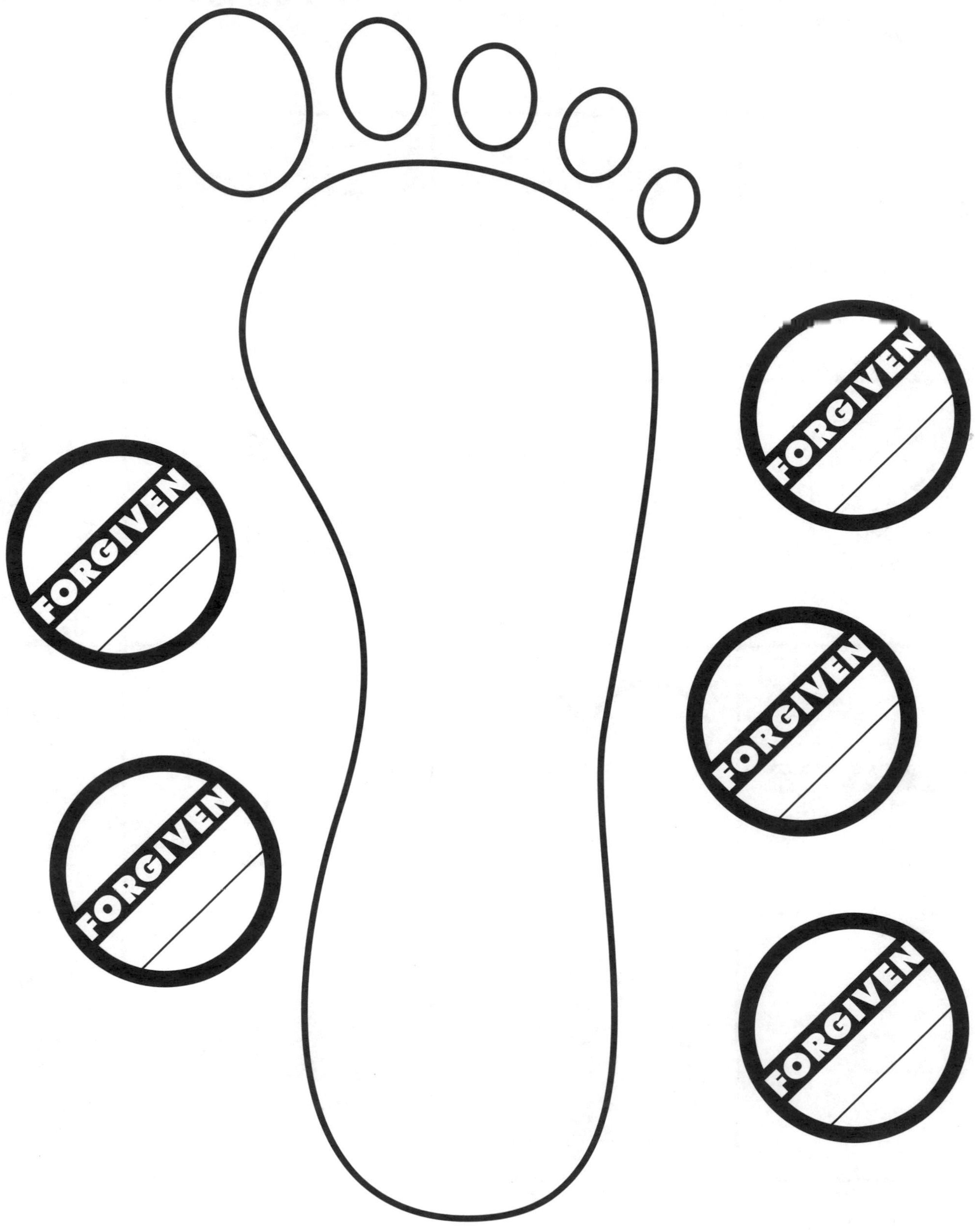

I want to follow in
Jesus' footsteps. He is my leader!

	John 3:16	but	the
	that		that
		4	
believes			
in		His	 should
	only	have	

I am thankful that Jesus gives me freedom from sin. He forgives me for the times when I do not want to worship or hear His Word.

How do you feel, knowing you are forgiven? Write a short thank-You prayer.

Dear Jesus,

____

____

____

____

In Your name I pray. Amen.

With the help of the Holy Spirit, we cheerfully listen to God's Word.

Draw a picture of yourself cheerfully listening to God's Word at home, church, or school. Add family members or friends to your picture.

Unit 6

Words to Remember

41. All have sinned and fall short of the glory of God. Romans 3:23

42. Surely He has borne our griefs and carried our sorrows. Isaiah 53:4

43. Fear not, for I have redeemed you; I have called you by name, you are Mine. Isaiah 43:1

44. We love because He first loved us. 1 John 4:19

45. May the Lord of peace Himself give you peace at all times in every way. 2 Thessalonians 3:16

46. He heals the brokenhearted and binds up their wounds. Psalm 147:3

47. [Jesus said], "I am the bread of life." John 6:35

48. Oh give thanks to the LORD, for He is good. Psalm 118:1

Dear Parents,

Does your child have a favorite superhero? Your child will naturally be drawn to Jesus' dynamic, spectacular displays of power in these Bible stories. These miracles may seem unbelievable, but God's Word is true, unlike many of the things your child sees on television. Your child will learn about Jesus healing a lame man at Bethesda, Jesus healing Peter's mother-in-law from a fever, Jesus helping Peter and his companions to catch boatloads of fish, Jesus healing a man with a withered hand, Jesus commanding the forces of nature, Jesus bringing a little girl back to life, Jesus feeding an enormous number of people with just a small amount of food, and Jesus healing men from leprosy. All of these miracles show how Jesus is true God, how Jesus has compassion and mercy on God's children, and how Jesus is even more powerful than sin, the devil, and death itself.

Just as the people in the Bible stories trusted in Jesus for help and healing, your child will learn that Jesus is our source for strength and comfort. Jesus cares for our every need, both physical and spiritual.

Read the stories in the book *Jesus' Miracles* with your child and marvel together at Jesus' love and power. Share with your child your own stories of how God has had mercy on you and has done some amazing things in your life. Remind each other that because there is sin in the world, we will face hardships, but because Jesus loves us, we will never face them alone, for our powerful God is with us always.

Sharing the love of Jesus,
Your child's teacher

Assessment: Unit 6

Write the following phrase on a piece of paper and photocopy for each child: "WOW! LOOK WHAT JESUS CAN DO!" Inside the *o*'s, students can draw pictures of four miracles they can remember. To make it a small-group project, write the phrase on chart paper, have students brainstorm a list of all the miracles they can remember, and then each child in the group can draw a larger picture of one miracle inside their own *o*. To make it a classroom project, write the phrase on butcher block paper. Students can draw their own favorite scenes from four different miracles on separate paper, cut them out, and then add one to each *o*, creating a collage inside each one.

Review the Unit 6 Word Wall Words. Encourage students to use as many as they can in journal writing.

Give students an opportunity to reveal what they remember about a story by doing a soliloquy. Use a simple prop or costume to help them dress up like a disciple or the person who was healed. He or she can tell others what amazing thing Jesus just did! Another option is to help students create paper lunch bag puppets of a character. Instead of the student acting out the role of one of the characters, the puppet does the re-telling of the story.

Have students work with their parents on a culminating activity. Can students ask their parents, grandparents, or neighbors if they have ever heard of a miracle happening today—something that defies the laws of nature? If every student brings back five written examples, your class could compile a list of a hundred miracles for the Hundredth Day of School! If you'd prefer an individual assessment, see how many biblical miracles (including Old Testament ones) students can write or speak in one hundred seconds.

Have students create a flap book. Each child can choose their favorite four stories to draw and/or write about. Fold a piece of paper in half horizontally. Cut the top half into four equal sections, cutting only to the fold. On this top (front) flap, students will write and/or draw the problem in the story. When the flap is flipped up, on the inside (bottom section) students will write and/or draw how Jesus took care of the person.

Have children pick a character and draw a picture of him or her. Then cut it out, cutting around the edge of the character, as if cropping around the outline of an image. Glue the image onto the left side of a half sheet of paper. In the remaining space on the paper, students can write what they know about the person. For a challenge, encourage students to make a simple poem using only adjectives or adjective phrases (show a sample).

Play Jeopardy as a whole class, with three teams, or have students write or say all the answers (questions) individually, so that you have an accurate assessment of their comprehension.

Lesson 41: What was wrong with him? ($100) Where did he sit? ($200) Why couldn't he get better? ($300) What did Jesus do? ($400)

Lesson 42: What was wrong? ($100) Where was she? ($200) What did she do when she got better? ($300) What did Jesus do? ($400)

Lesson 43: Whose boat did Jesus get into to preach? ($100) Where was the boat? ($200) Why was Peter frustrated? ($300) What did Jesus do? ($400)

Lesson 44: What does *withered* mean? ($100) Where was he? ($200) What day was it, which made the Pharisees so mad? ($300) What did Jesus do? ($400)

Lesson 45: What happened to the lake and boat? ($100) Where was the boat? ($200) What was Jesus doing during the storm? ($300) What did Jesus do when He woke up? ($400)

Lesson 46: What was wrong with Jairus's daughter? ($100) Where was the girl? ($200) Whom did Jesus heal along the way to her house? ($300) What did Jesus do when He got there? ($400)

Lesson 47: What was the problem? ($100) Where was the crowd? ($200) What did Jesus ask the disciples to do? ($300) What did Jesus do? ($400)

Lesson 48: What is leprosy? ($100) Where were the lepers? ($200) What was different about the leper from Samaria? ($300) What did Jesus do for the lepers? ($400)

Make up a game with a new set of dice. Choose six of the eight stories. Perhaps you can reduce the image at the top of each student page. Glue the images to the sides of a dice pattern (see Web Resource Unit 6a), then fold the edges and glue the flaps together to create a die. Divide children into small groups. Call out a story element (e.g., setting, characters, problem, solution, etc.). Children can take turns rolling the die and giving that information about the story they rolled. As they verbalize what they recall, take anecdotal notes about their descriptions.

Jesus Heals a Crippled Man

John 5:1–18

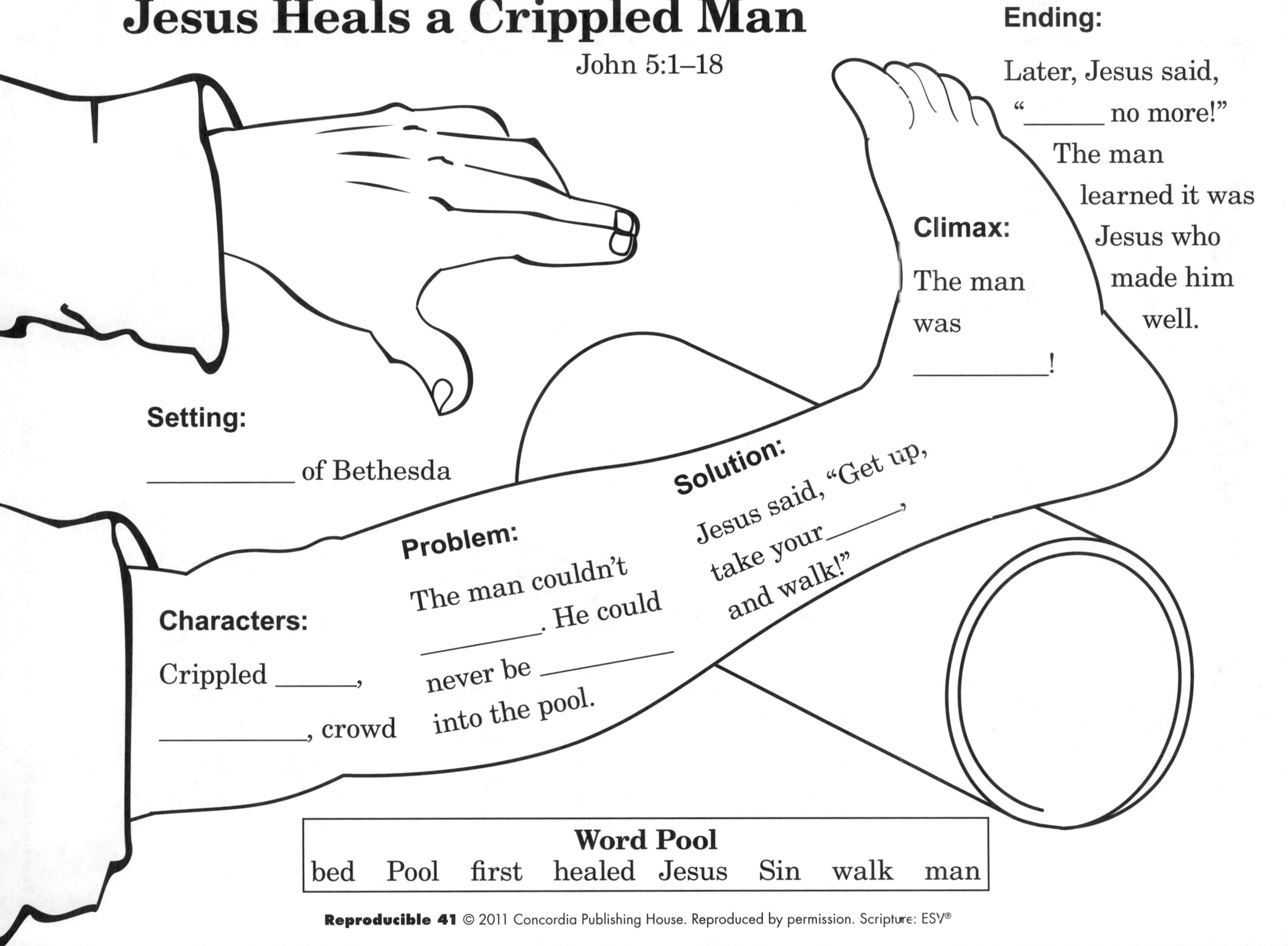

Setting:

__________ of Bethesda

Characters:

Crippled ______,
__________, crowd

Problem:

The man couldn't
________. He could
never be __________
into the pool.

Solution:

Jesus said, "Get up,
take your ______,
and walk!"

Climax:

The man
was
__________!

Ending:

Later, Jesus said,
"______ no more!"
The man
learned it was
Jesus who
made him
well.

Word Pool							
bed	Pool	first	healed	Jesus	Sin	walk	man

I feel better. Now what?

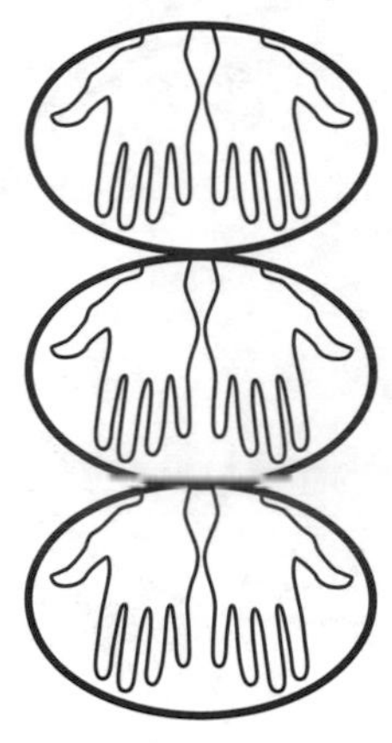

1. Pick up your toys.

2. Throw gravel on the playground.

3. Push the button on the remote to choose the TV show you want to watch.

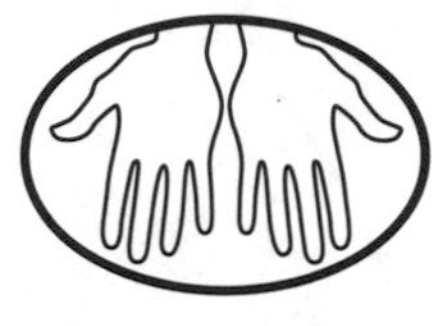

4. Stir food for mom or dad to help with supper.

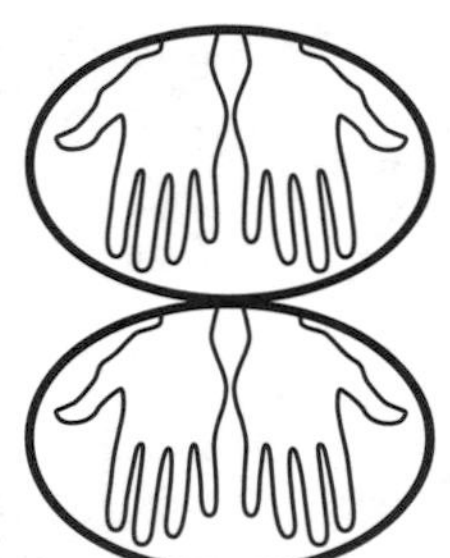

5. Set out the napkins for dinner.

6. Push your little brother when he's in your way when you're trying to play your game.

7. Punch someone in your class when they call you a name.

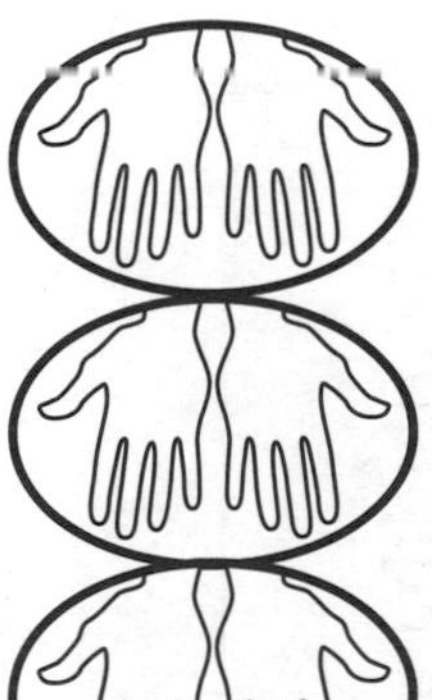

8. Say a thank-You prayer.

9. Push a friend on the swings.

10. Get your mom or dad a drink out of the fridge.

Who Can You Catch with Jesus' Love?

Reach Out and Show You Care

How can you show someone you care in each of these settings? Draw a picture or write your ideas.

Home

School

Jesus Stills the Storm

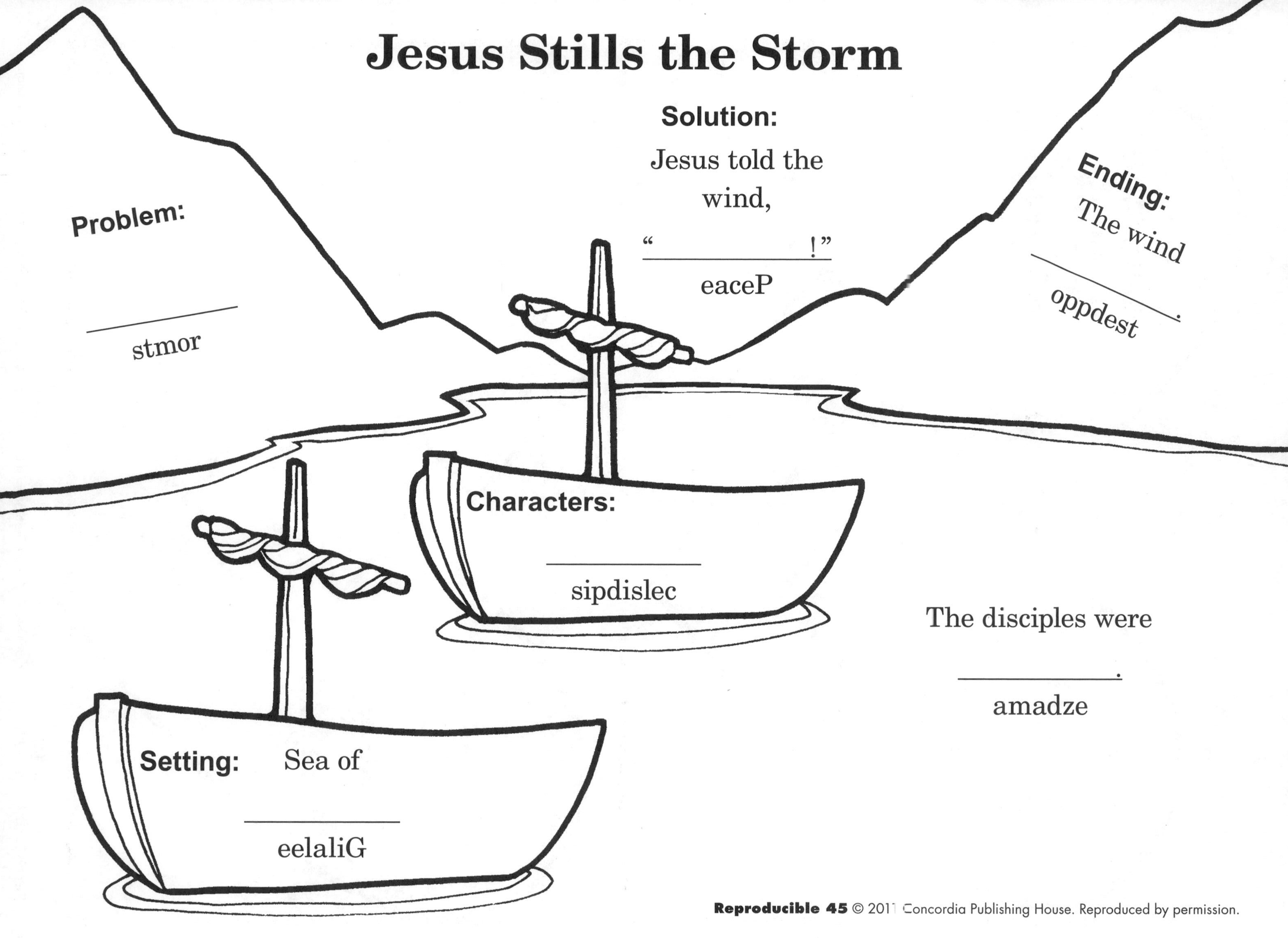

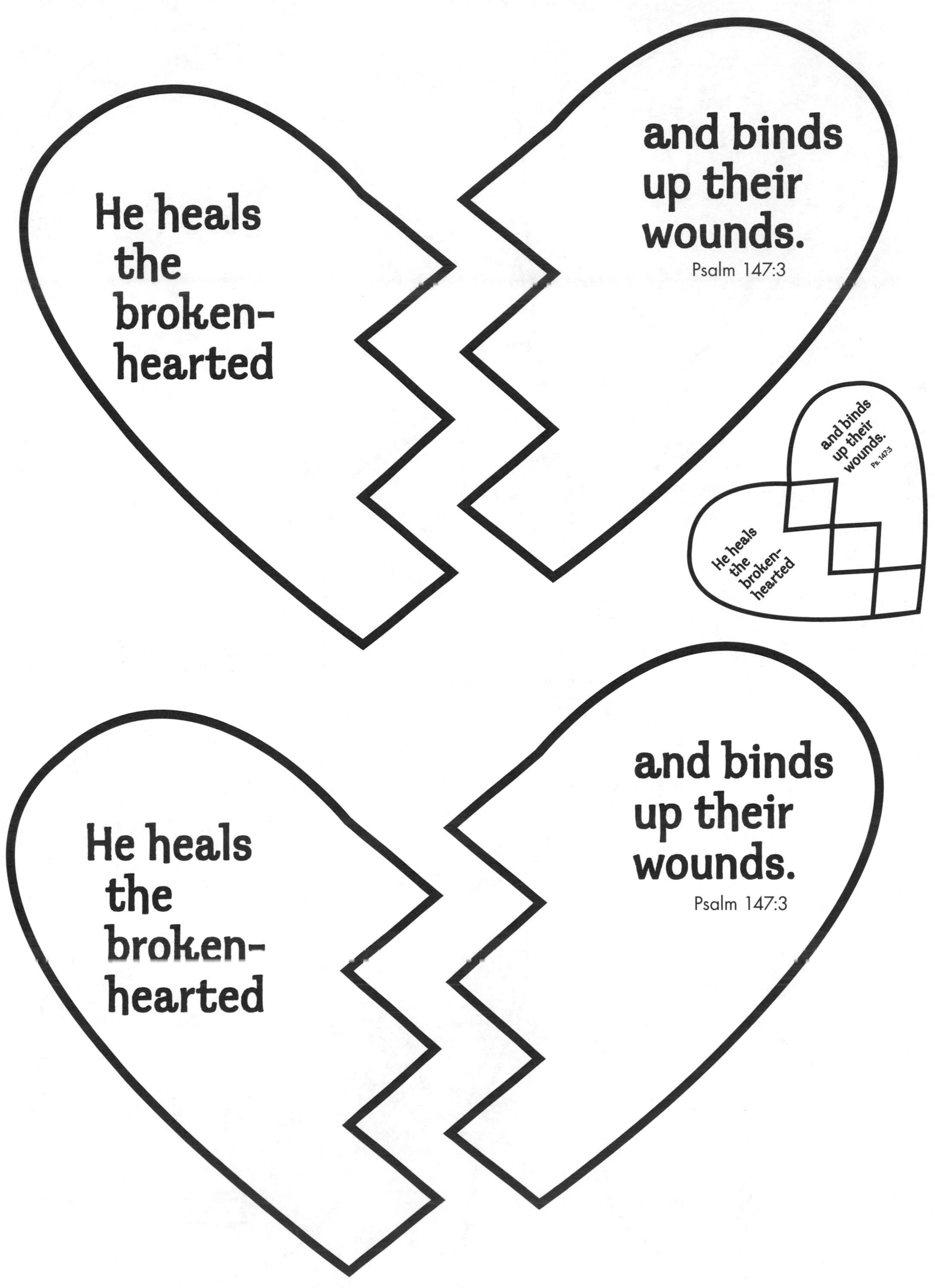
He heals
the
broken-
hearted
and binds
up their
wounds.
Psalm 147:3
and binds
up their
wounds.
Ps. 147:3
He heals
the
broken-
hearted
He heals
the
broken-
hearted
and binds
up their
wounds.
Psalm 147:3

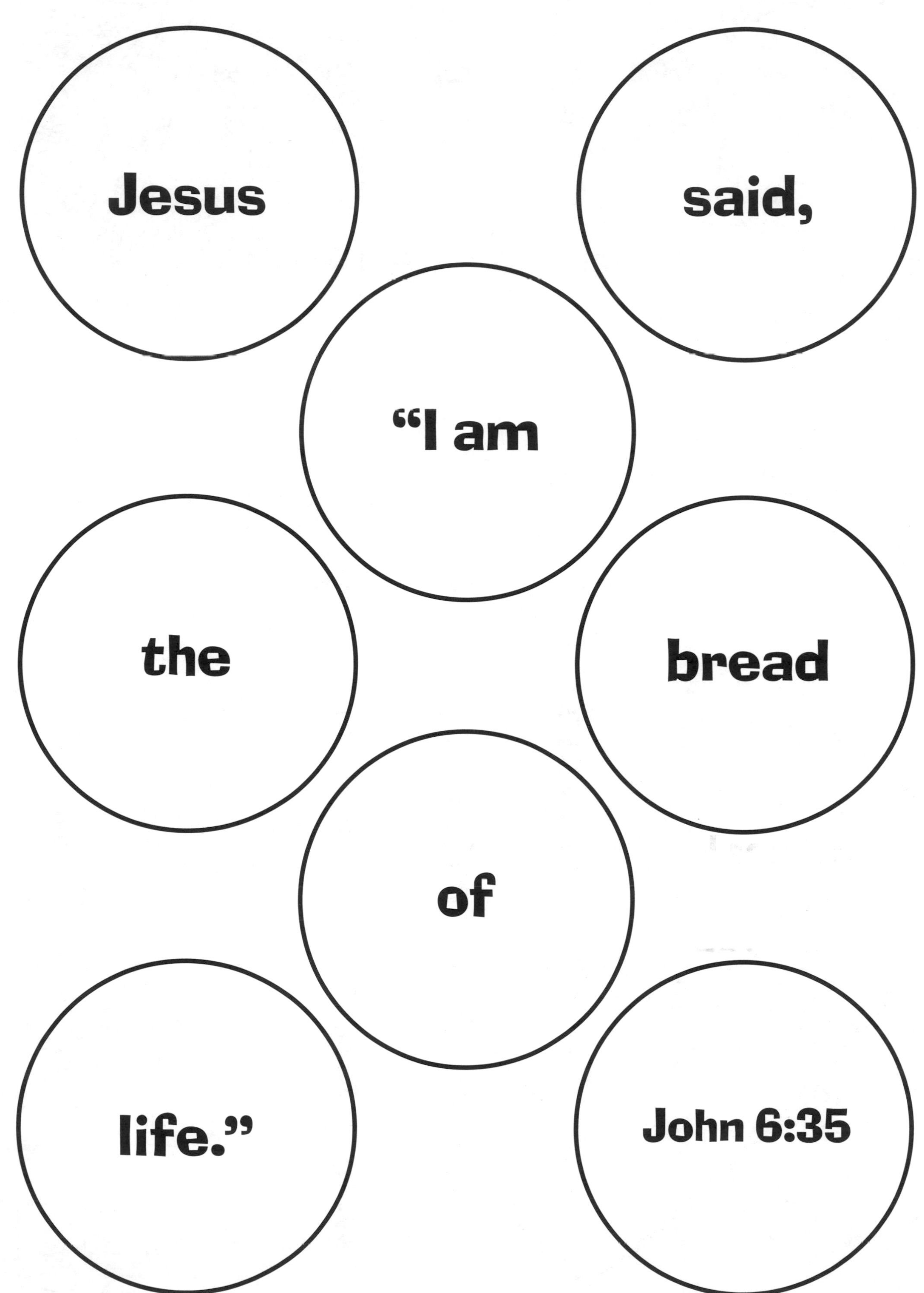
Jesus
said,
“I am
the
bread
of
life.”
John 6:35

For ______________________, thank You, loving Father.

For ______________________, thank You, loving Father.

For ______________________, thank You, loving Father.

For ______________________, thank You, loving Father.

For ______________________, thank You, loving Father.

Unit 7

Words to Remember

49. "Fear not, little flock, for it is your Father's good pleasure to give you the kingdom." Luke 12:32

50. For by grace you have been saved through faith. . . . [I]t is the gift of God, not a result of works, so that no one may boast. Ephesians 2:8–9

51. "Your Father knows what you need before you ask Him." Matthew 6:8

52. "The Son of Man came to seek and to save the lost." Luke 19:10

53. The Lord is gracious and compassionate, slow to anger and rich in love. Psalm 145:8 NIV

54. "God, be merciful to me, a sinner!" Luke 18:13

55. These are written so that you may believe that Jesus is the Christ, the Son of God. John 20:31

56. "To love [Jesus] with all the heart and with all the understanding and with all the strength . . . is much more than all . . . offerings and sacrifices." Mark 12:33

Dear Parents,

In the last unit, your child learned about God's power through Jesus' miracles. Jesus also taught His disciples, crowds, and even people today through His preaching. Jesus tried to explain the kingdom of God (of heaven) to His listeners. Our stories will focus on Jesus' main themes of God's love, care, and forgiveness. As we are God's children, living under Him in His kingdom, we learn to trust in His care and protection, and we learn to honor Him and put Him first in our lives.

Here is what your child will learn from the stories:

- "Jesus Teaches Not to Worry": God doesn't want His children to worry, but to trust in Him.
- "The Rich Young Ruler": God knows His children can't keep His rules, so He sent Jesus to secure our salvation.
- "The Parable of the Rich Fool": God wants His children to let go of their selfish desires and to put loving God and others first.
- "The Parable of the Lost Sheep": Like a good shepherd, Jesus saves those who aren't following Him.
- "The Parable of the Lost Son": Like a loving father, God forgives everyone—no matter what they've done.
- "The Parable of the Pharisee and the Tax Collector": God wants His children to have be humble, but also to rejoice that they are forgiven.
- "Jesus Raises Lazarus": God wants His children to have the hope of new life through Jesus.
- "Mary Anoints Jesus": God wants His children to love Him with their whole heart.

There's no doubt that Jesus' words can be hard to understand, for children *and* adults. Jesus often told stories called "parables," which had a double (heavenly) meaning. Before you read the Bible or listen to a sermon, pray that the Holy Spirit would give you understanding. Don't let frustration stop you; the more you study God's Word, the more you will understand how great our heavenly Father's love is for you. Read the stories in the book *Jesus Speaks to the People* with your child, and pray that he or she will begin to understand the treasure of heaven and the riches we have only through the grace of Jesus Christ. May we all diligently strive to place God and His kingdom first in our lives.

Sharing the love of Jesus,
Your child's teacher

Assessment: Unit 7

What's the "moral" to the story? Make a list of the parables in this unit. Leave room for the students to write a sentence or two about what they think Jesus was trying to teach with the story. Accept reasonable answers.

Review the Unit 7 Word Wall Words. Encourage students to use as many as they can in journal writing.

Give students time to create their own picture storybook modeled after *David Goes to School* by David Shannon. Staple folded pages together for a book and let them choose a title such as *[Child's name] Goes [location of their choice, e.g., "to School," "Home," "to Church," "to the Grocery," etc.].* Have students write and draw *at least two* examples of how they have made bad choices and gotten into trouble, straying from their heavenly Father. Be sure they include the consequences of their behavior, such as when David had to stay after school. Ask, **What punishment did you receive from a parent or other adult?** Finally, be sure students include an example of grace and forgiveness at the end, such as when the teacher told David "Good job!" and let him go home. If they *didn't* experience forgiveness, have them draw what they wish *would* have happened. Do your students seem to understand how they are sometimes like the lost sheep or lost son and how God is like the seeking shepherd and forgiving father?

Can students think of selfish, greedy thoughts that choke out thoughts about God—things that take time away from loving others or spending time in God's Word? Give them time to individually brainstorm things that can get in the way of loving God. Ask, **What things are you tempted to love and spend more time with than God? What things would you rather be doing than loving others and worshiping God or reading the Bible?** Do your students understand how they stray from God and are sometimes greedy, do what they want, or are even self-righteous and don't think they need God?

Then play a game of tag. The tagger is "Jesus." You may want this student to wear a necklace or sticker/label that lists what He's trying to give His children (forgiveness of sins, life, salvation). But the children are like the lost lamb or lost son—they run away from Jesus and His blessings and want to do their own things. If the children see Jesus coming, they sit down and say one of their brainstormed ideas in order to be "safe" from Jesus' tag. If Jesus does tag a child, he or she becomes a member of God's kingdom/family and joyfully skips around, telling the other children to get up and let Jesus call them into His family—but they continue to refuse Jesus' love and run away. Play until almost all the children are called to be God's children. Give other children the opportunity to pretend to be Jesus.

Play a matching game using the following phrases to create a worksheet or sentence strips that students can align on a pocket chart. Make three cards for each character: his or her name, a paraphrase of what he or she said during the story, and a possibility of what he or she *might* have said after the experience. If using both phrases, you may want to only list half of the characters at a time.

Rich Young Ruler: "What good deed must I do to inherit eternal life?"; "*We* can't earn salvation. It's a gift from God."

Rich Fool: "I will eat, relax, and be merry"; "I wish I wouldn't have thought only about being rich and spending money."

Lost Sheep: "I want to go off by myself"; "I wish I would have stayed close to the shepherd."

Lost Son: "Give me my share of the inheritance"; "Father, I have sinned against heaven and against you."

Pharisee: "I'm glad I'm not like that sinner over there"; "I wish I would have realized that I'm a sinner and need Jesus' forgiveness."

Martha: "Jesus, if You had been here, my brother would not have died"; "I know to have hope and trust that Jesus knows best."

Disciples: "She shouldn't have used that up. She could have given the money to the poor"; "We realize she was showing love and worshiping Jesus. It was the right thing to do."

Some children express themselves (and their understanding/recall of the story) well through acting. Do not provide scripts. Divide children into small groups and assign each a story. Or you may prefer to have students work independently. Ask, **Which character do you think you're most like?** Can students identify with a character? Give them choices so they remember (e.g., the rich farmer, who doesn't recognize that his gifts are from God and doesn't spend time with God; Martha, who knows Jesus is the Christ, but still forgot to have hope; Mary, who kept to herself and mourned privately; the sheep that ran away; the sheep that stayed in the pen; the lost son, who made bad choices; the older brother, who didn't think grace is fair; the Pharisee or rich ruler, who thinks he is behaving okay; the tax collector, who feels sorry for his sins; Mary, who would give up anything for Jesus; or the disciples, who don't quite understand why loving Jesus is more important than anything else). Can they pretend to be that character, retelling what they did and why?

Use a plastic pot (e.g., something found around Halloween time or one found in a garden center) and real, plastic, or candy coins. Listen to students create their own "pot of gold" by tossing coins into the pot, naming a blessing from God each time. You may want to have students do the activity individually or in small groups; then form a line, having each student continue to take a turn and go to the end of the line until the pot is full, the coins are gone, or the students can't think of any more examples. As our stories warn, it's a temptation to be greedy and selfish, so it's good to consider what we *do* have through Christ. We have more riches than the wealthiest people on earth because we are God's children through faith. The Bible calls it the riches of God's grace. Do your students remember to mention our family inheritance—heaven and the forgiveness of sins?

Do not worry about what you will
________. Your Father knows
you need food.

Do not worry about what you wil[l]
________. Your Father knows yo[u]
need clothes.

Seek first His
________________.

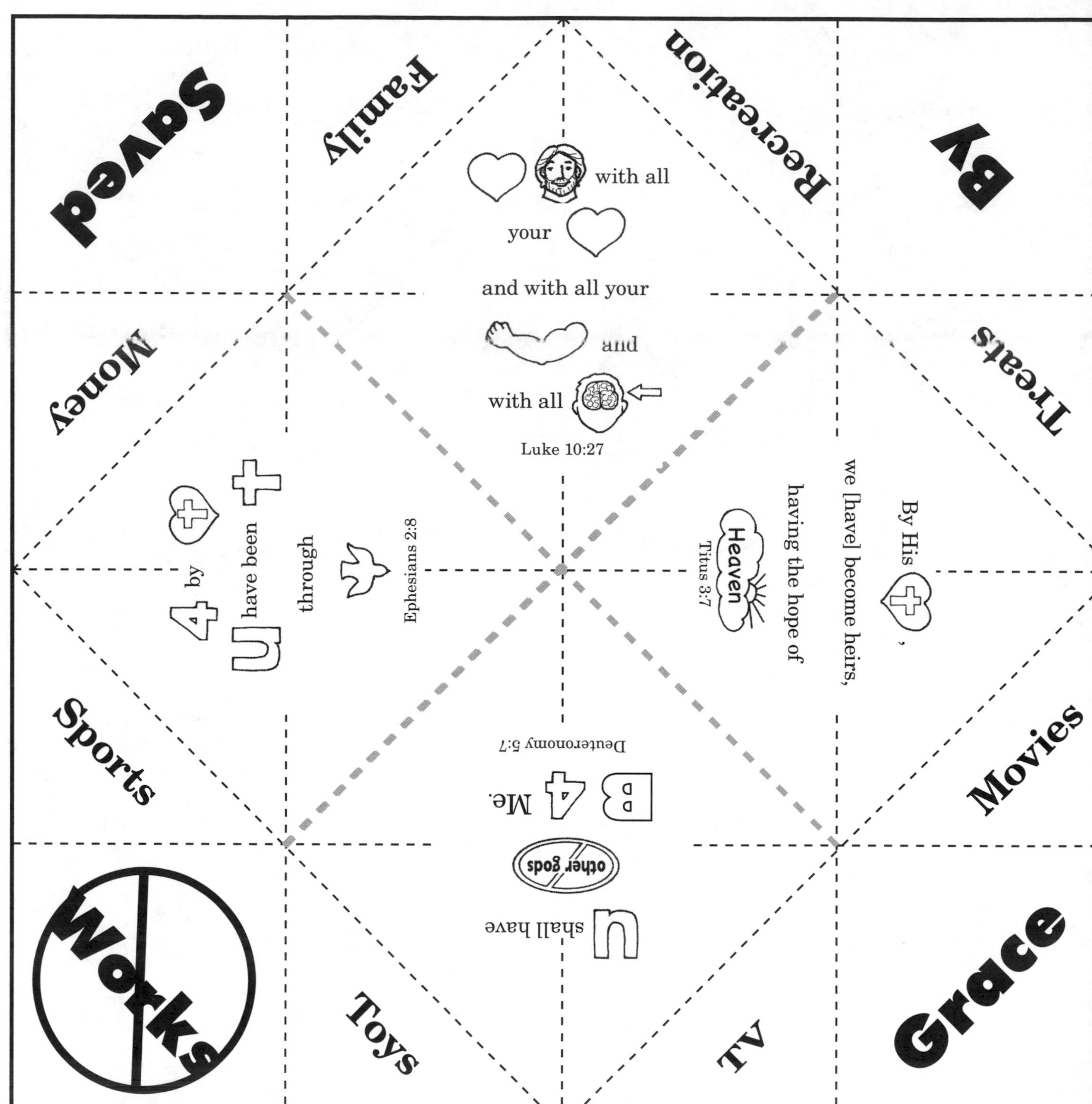

Instructions:

1. Cut out along the solid outline.
2. Flip. Fold back 4 triangular corners.
3. Flip. Fold 4 corners to center, so 8 words show.
4. Fold in half with Words to Remember facing out.
5. Put your thumbs and pointer fingers under the four flaps.

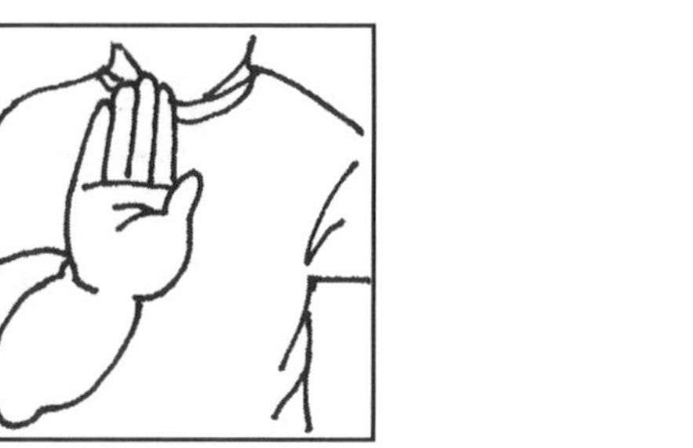
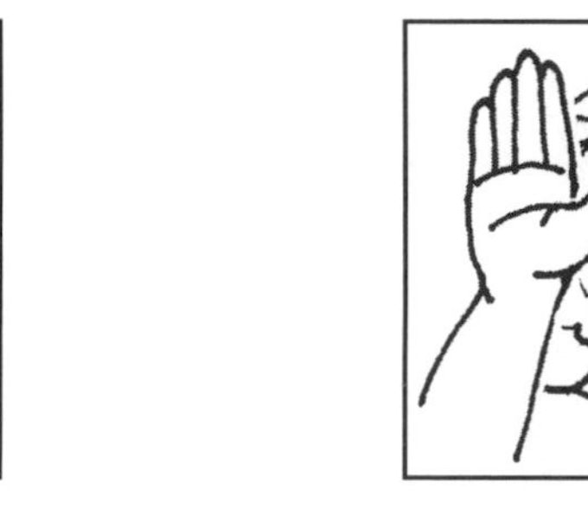

Your

____

knows

what

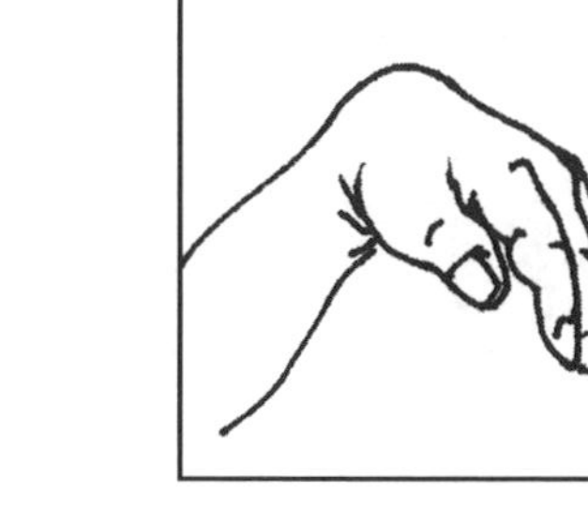
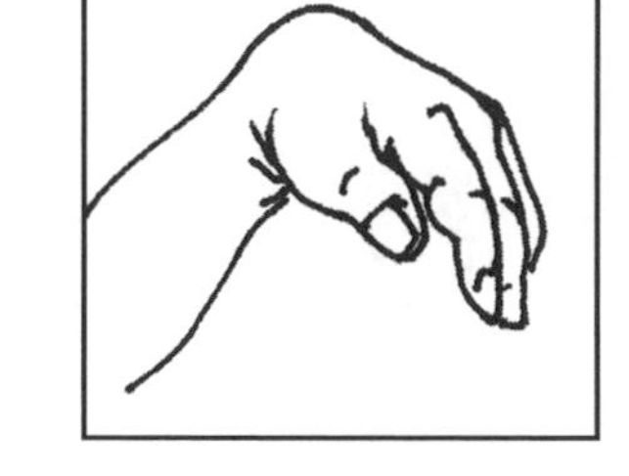

you

need

before

you

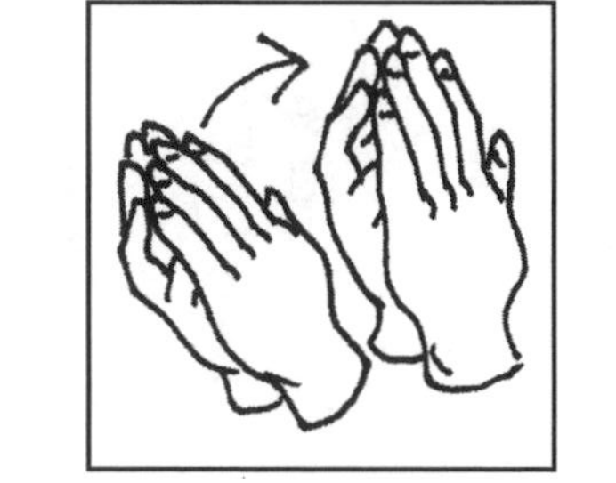

ask

Him.

Matthew 6:8

You repent for not telling the truth. Go **1** space.	You repent for not writing your grandparents a letter. Go **1** space.	You repent for not helping your mom with the baby. Go **1** space.
You repent for not helping your mom and dad with chores. Go **2** spaces.	You repent for not inviting someone to Sunday School. Go **2** spaces.	You repent for not keeping the Ten Commandments. Go **1** space.
You repent for not taking out the trash like your parents asked. Go **2** spaces.	You tell a lie. Go back **1** space.	You don't help your brother with his homework. Go back **1** space.
You repent for not helping a person in need. Go **2** spaces.	You repent for teasing your little brother. Go **1** space.	You repent for not inviting a new girl to play with you at school. Go **2** spaces.
You break a promise. Go back **1** space.	You don't share your snack with a friend. Go back **2** spaces.	You repent for not praying for missionaries. Go **1** space.
You repent for not helping your mom take cookies to the new neighbor. Go **1** space.	You push your sister. Go back **1** space.	You repent for not giving an offering to Jesus. Go **1** space.
You repent for not showing kindness to a lonely person. Go **2** spaces.	You repent for not speaking kindly of an unpopular student at school. Go **2** spaces.	You repent for not singing praises to Jesus. Go **1** space.
You disobey your parents. Go back **1** space.	You repent for not sending a card to a sick relative. Go **2** spaces.	You take a cookie without asking. Go back **1** space.

A-maz-ing Love!

What does the LORD require of you?

a	b	c	d	e
g	h	i	j	k
l	m	n	o	r
s	t	u	v	w
y				

_ o   _ o   _ u _ _ i _ e

a _ _   _ o   _ o _ e

_ i _ _ _ e _ _   a _ _   _ o

_ a _ _   _ u _ _ _ _   _ i _ _

_ o u _   _ o _

Jesus Raises Lazarus

Narrator: Jesus was with His disciples when He received an important message.

Messenger: Lord, Mary and Martha sent me to tell You that Lazarus, the one You love, is really sick!

Jesus: This sickness will not end in death. I will show you once again that I am God's Son. We must go back to Judea.

Disciples: But Lord, some of the people there want to hurt You!

Jesus: It will be okay.

Narrator: Now, Lazarus did die, and Jesus did go back to Judea. When He saw Mary and Martha, they all cried. They knew that death was not a good thing.

Mary and Martha: If You could have been here, I know our brother would not have died.

Jesus: Your brother will rise again!

Martha: I know he will rise again in the resurrection on the Last Day.

Jesus: I am the resurrection and the life. Anyone who believes in Me will live even after he dies. Do you believe this?

Martha: I believe that You are the Christ, the Son of God!

Jesus: Now, tell Me, where have you laid Lazarus?

Mary and Martha: Come and see, Lord.

Narrator: Jesus went to the tomb where Lazarus had been for four days. He said to the people,

Jesus: Take away the stone.

Martha: But, Lord, he is dead.

Jesus: If you believe, you will see the glory of God.

Narrator: So the people took the stone away. Then Jesus, after thanking God for letting Him show God's glory, shouted,

Jesus: Lazarus, come out!

Narrator: Lazarus came out of the tomb, and the people rejoiced, for this man who had been dead was alive again.

This certificate is good for

____

To ______________________

From ______________________

This certificate is good for

____

To ______________________

From ______________________

This certificate is good for

____

To ______________________

From ______________________

Unit 8

Words to Remember

57. Christ Jesus came into the world to save sinners. 1 Timothy 1:15

58. Make a joyful noise to the LORD, all the earth! Psalm 100:1

59. Greater love has no one than this, that someone lay down his life for his friends. John 15:13

60. Watch and pray that you may not enter into temptation. Matthew 26:41

61. If we confess our sins, He is faithful and just to forgive us our sins. 1 John 1:9

62. The LORD has laid on [Jesus] the iniquity of us all. Isaiah 53:6

63. Truly, I say to you, today you will be with Me in Paradise. Luke 23:43

64. Let us continually offer up a sacrifice of praise to God . . . lips that acknowledge His name. Hebrews 13:15

Dear Parents,

Your child will be learning about the events leading up to and through Holy Week (Palm Sunday through Good Friday). Easter will begin our next unit. These are the most pivotal events in all of human history because Jesus defeated death forever. “If Christ has not been raised, your faith is futile and you are still in your sins” (1 Corinthians 15:17). This is why Jesus came into the world. This was God’s plan since the beginning of time—since the first sin. This is what your child has been studying all year: the story of God’s love, demonstrated in His plan of salvation as it is fulfilled in Jesus.

Jesus did what we couldn’t do for ourselves. He lived a perfect life; though innocent, He took the punishment for sin; and because He is true God, He came alive again after His death on the cross. When your child sees a cross and sees the bread and cup at Holy Communion, he or she will be reminded of Jesus’ great love, which brings forgiveness and salvation. Your child may respond to Jesus’ suffering with sadness that it was for *our* sins that He was hurt. It is when they are sorry for their sins that Jesus’ love and forgiveness means the most to them, personally.

With your child, respond to Jesus’ love by worshiping our Savior, showing love to others, and forgiving others as Jesus forgave. Through Baptism, your child is a son or daughter of the King who saves. May the joy of the children shouting “Hosanna!” (“Lord, save us!”) on Palm Sunday and the anticipation of the time when we will live in His heavenly kingdom fill you with hope each day. Read the stories in *Jesus Saves* with your child, and together give thanks that we did not have to bear the punishment for our sins.

Sharing the love of Jesus,
Your child’s teacher

Assessment: Unit 8

Provide symbol-shaped paper (a coat from Palm Sunday, a chalice, a cross, a tomb, etc.) to motivate your students to write about what Holy Week means to them. Some open-ended questions may provide a starting point: "Why did Jesus have to die on the cross?" "How does it make you feel that Jesus had to die?" "Why does it make you sad?" "Why does it make you happy?" "Why Is Jesus a King?" or "If I Were on Trial . . ." You may want to encourage students to use as many of the Unit 8 Word Wall Words as they can in their journal writing.

Make a video book to capture the events of Holy Week. Provide each student with a six- or seven-frame cartoon strip. Give students time to draw, in order, a picture of each Holy Week story that has been studied throughout the unit. The strip will fit as a pull tab through two slits of the same size on another piece of paper. This will form a "window." Only one scene will show at a time; the rest will be hidden behind the paper.
If desired, below the window, staple six or seven strips of paper. Students can write one sentence about each scene, turning the pages to match the frame showing above. This activity could easily be turned into one that uses technology. Scan the pictures and create a simple digital story.

Create a class book *What the Cross Means to Me*. Cut the silhouette of Jesus' cross on the hill into the top edge of all the pages, so the book has a defined shape. Give each child a page on which to share personal thoughts and color the Golgotha scene at the top of the page; bind together at the side.

Provide food prompts to initiate discussion about the stories. Ask students, **What story does this food remind you of? What do you remember about what happened?** Take notes about how well they recall the events in each story.

Palm Sunday: Provide spinach leaves for palm branches and use Ranch salad dressing to make the outline of a shirt (cloak) on a paper plate.

The Last Supper: Provide crackers and grape juice.

Jesus in Gethsemane: Provide olives, because Jesus prayed on the Mount of Olives.

Peter Denies Jesus: Provide two funnel-shaped corn snacks to form a rooster's beak. If students slide their thumb and index finger into the snacks and move their fingers, it will look like a beak opening and closing.

Jesus before Pilate: Use pull-and-peel licorice to form a whip. Poke several toothpicks in a chocolate, crumb, or coconut crunch miniature donut to create a crown of thorns.

Jesus on the Cross: Form a cross with graham cracker rectangles.

Jesus Dies and Is Buried: Use a small flour tortilla or thin white cheese slice (provolone or processed Swiss) for the burial linen. Use a vanilla wafer or donut hole to represent the stone rolled in front of the tomb.

Make a diorama-in-the-round. Provide students with two evenly cut tagboard circles. Help students to fold the circles in half. Show the students how to put both circles on a desk with two halves sitting on the desk and two halves up. Students will glue the vertical halves of the circles back-to-back. This creates the back of the diorama. The two halves on the desk that face out create two bases for the two-sided diorama. Give students time to create a "Good Friday" scene on one half. Save the other half to create an "Easter" scene on it during the next unit. Show students how to fold the bottom of a small piece of paper to glue to the base of the diorama, making the paper stand up and create upright people or other objects.

Make a step book. Overlap three sheets of 8 ½ × 11-inch paper, leaving a one-inch margin at the bottom of each page. Fold the top edge over, creating three more overlapping pages, also one inch apart. The book should have six pages, evenly spaced apart. At the fold, staple through all of the layers. The pages of the book can be flipped up, or the book can be turned sideways so the pages are turned to the left, not up. Write "Holy Week" on the outside of the top page. Students draw, in order, the events of Holy Week that they can recall.

Use Good Friday and Easter Arch Books. Pause at the end of the lines for students to complete the rhymes. Do they understand enough about the story to predict what word would make sense in context?

Create a character from one of the stories (Zacchaeus, Peter, Judas, etc.) using a paper plate. Write a main idea about that person on his or her nose. Display the characters in the hallway, allowing other students to read the information clue and guess the person's name. The answer (character's name) can be written on a one-inch wide strip of paper, attached securely to the character's mouth on the paper plate, as if a tongue. If students wrap the end of the strip around a pencil and roll it up, the tongue will have some curl.

Give students time to respond to Jesus' amazing love by writing a song of praise with a partner or small group. Use Web Resource Unit 8a to help children compose.

Create a Holy Week Word Wall or bulletin board. Use Web Resource Unit 8b to match words with the days of Jesus' last week or print out the words. Create your own strips or index cards for students to categorize. Give them time to draw corresponding images, creating a class "Lenten Picture Dictionary."

Lord, Save Us!

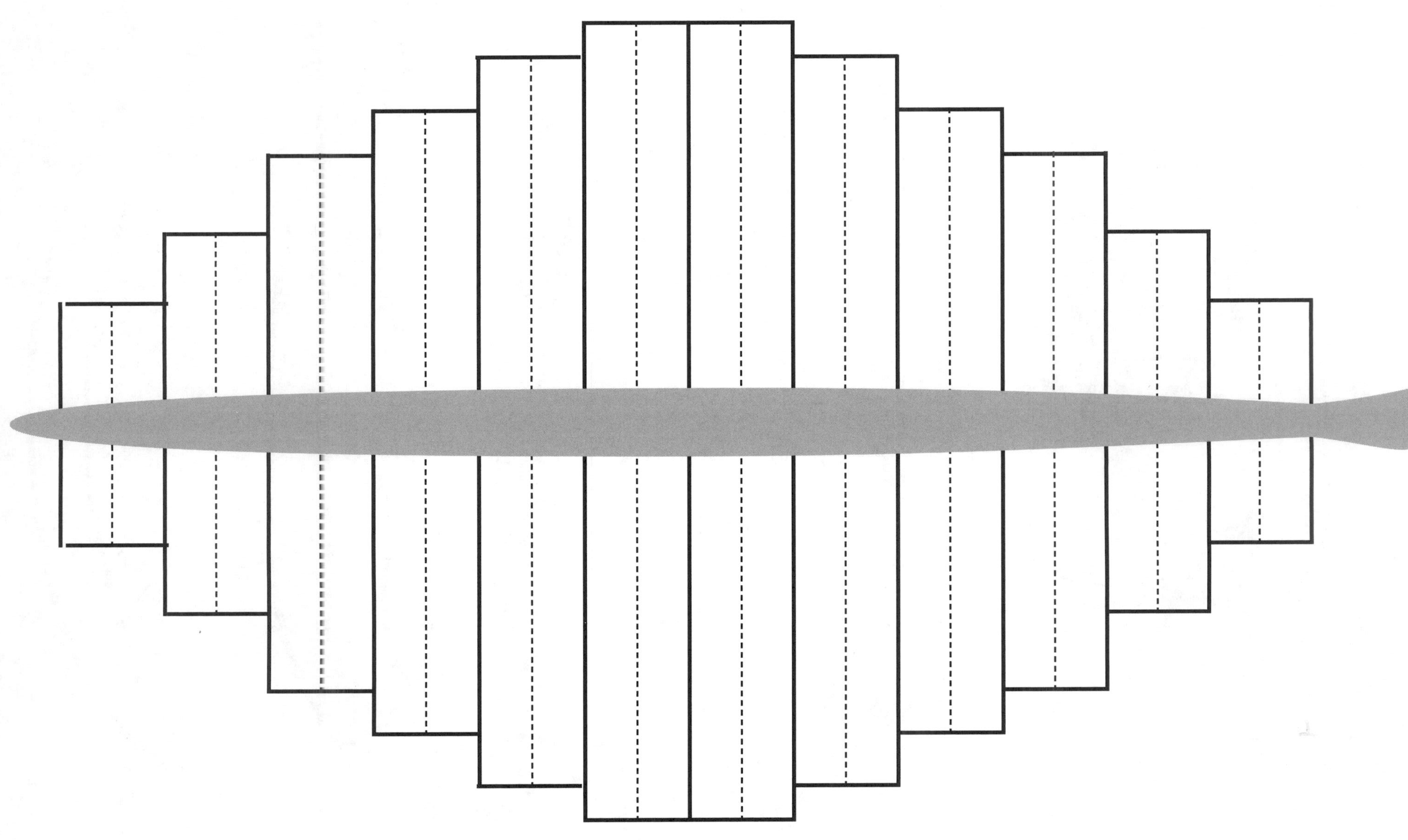

The Special Meal

(Sung to the tune of "Jesus Loves Me")

Jesus' work was almost done—
What God had planned since time
begun.
He fed the crowds and healed the lame.
He lived His life without a blame.

Refrain:
Yes, Jesus loves me,
Yes, Jesus loves me,
Yes, Jesus loves me
The Bible tells me so!

Gathered for the special meal
Were His friends so He could heal
All their hurts and sad regrets.
With His life He'd pay their debts.

Refrain

"Take and eat," He broke the bread,
Passed it to His friends and said,
"This is My body giv'n for you,
Think of Me each time you do."

Refrain

Then He took a cup of wine,
Said, "Please come and with Me dine."
The price of all our sins He'll lift.
Take and drink; receive this gift.

Refrain

Lamb of God, please take away
All the sin in me today.
Help me to be kind and good.
Help me do the things I should.

Refrain

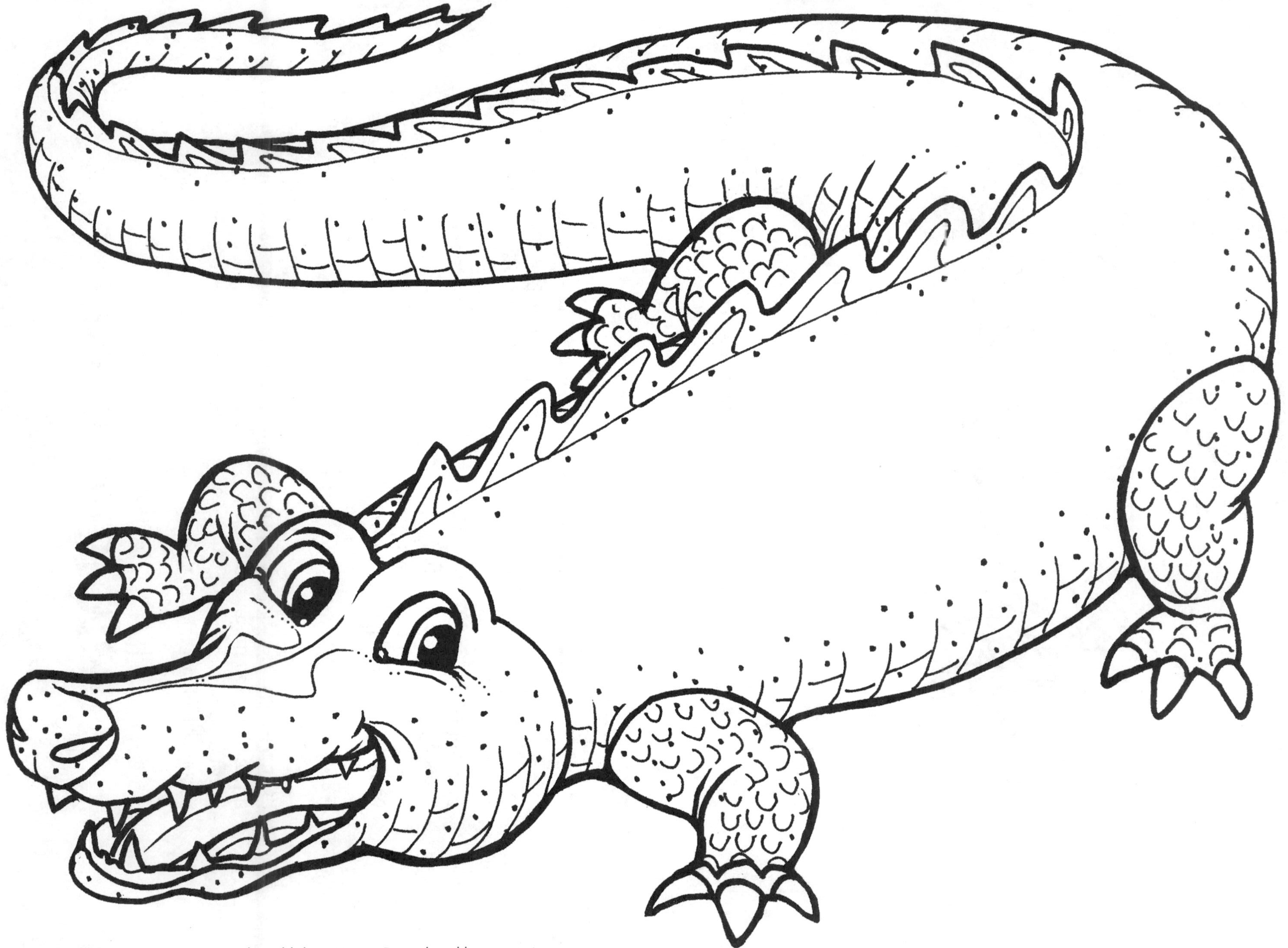

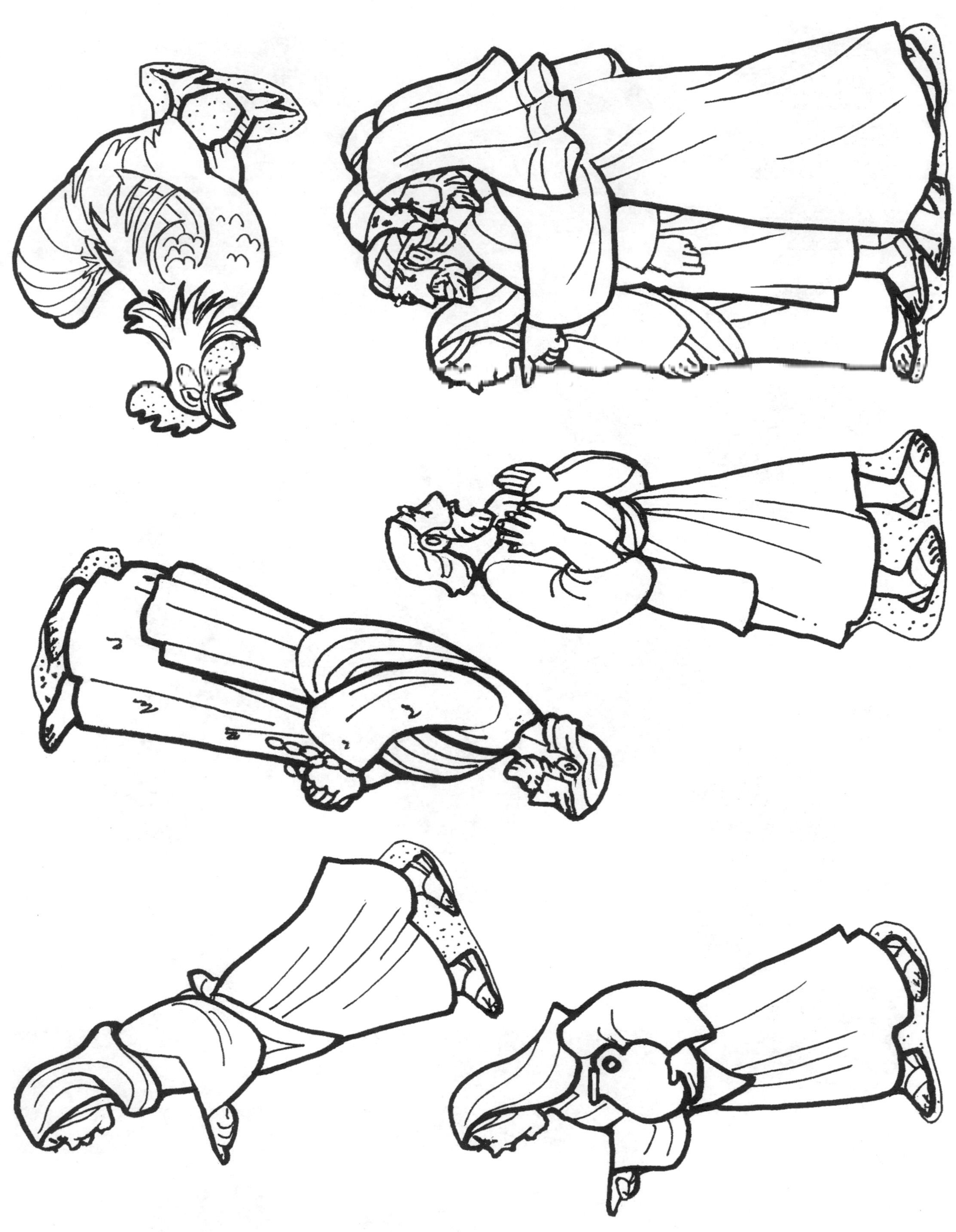

Suncatcher

1. Place the pattern under a clear, plastic lid.
2. Use permanent markers to trace the symbol.
3. Use lighter colored markers to add large mosaic tiles (like a stained glass window) for the background.
4. Punch a hole at the top. Hang.

Reproducible 64

Unit 9

Words to Remember

65. Do not be afraid, for I know that you seek Jesus who was crucified. He is not here, for He has risen. Matthew 28:5–6

66. I know that my Redeemer lives. Job 19:25

67. Your word is a lamp to my feet and a light to my path. Psalm 119:105

68. [Jesus said,] "I am with you always." Matthew 28:20

69. Faith comes from hearing, and hearing through the word of Christ. Romans 10:17

70. For I am not ashamed of the gospel, for it is the power of God for salvation to everyone who believes. Romans 1:16

71. Continue in what you have learned and have firmly believed. 2 Timothy 3:14

72. See what kind of love the Father has given to us, that we should be called children of God. 1 John 3:1

Dear Parents,

Your child's last unit ended with the story of Jesus' death and burial. This unit is all about the Good News that Jesus rose from the dead, defeating sin, death, and the devil! Your child will learn the Easter story from the perspective of some of Jesus' disciples (the women, Mary Magdalene, and the disciples from the town of Emmaus). The unit is all about sharing the message that Jesus has saved us. Your child will see how Jesus promised to be with His disciples (including us) forever and gave them (and us) the gift of the Holy Spirit. The Holy Spirit gives us the power to tell others about Jesus. Your child will see how the apostle Paul, Timothy, and Tabitha shared the love of Jesus.

Praise your child for showing the love of Jesus through his or her actions—being caring, sharing, and loving. Praise your child for showing the love of Jesus through words—telling others what he or she believes about Jesus or sharing with others how Jesus is with them every day. Ask the Holy Spirit to help you be a witness to your child, sharing Jesus' love with your own words and actions. If you don't know what you believe about Jesus, ask the Holy Spirit to strengthen your faith through God's Word. Read the stories in the *Tell about Jesus* book with your child. See how the Holy Spirit gives believers the power to lead a life that witnesses boldly to God's love and grace through Jesus Christ.

Sharing the love of Jesus,
Your child's teacher

Assessment: Unit 9

Review the Unit 9 Word Wall Words. Encourage students to use as many as they can in journal writing.

Make a classroom bulletin board entitled "God Cares and We Share." Children can trace their hands on construction paper and then cut them out. On the palm of the hand, they should write one way that God cares for them. On each finger, they should write a different way that they can share love with others. You may want to place the hands around the outside edge of the Unit 9 Bulletin Board available from Concordia Publishing House. The hands would create an attractive, correlated frame with those images.

Take silly individual pictures of your students with two Pringles chips in their mouths, making their mouths look like large lips or a duck's beak. Post the pictures in the hallway alongside the student's short, open-ended essay entitled "What I Want to Tell People about Jesus." This could also easily become a digital story. Record the students reading their essay (or just talking about what they would say about Jesus); coordinate the audio with the individual pictures. Give parents a copy of this keepsake classroom testimony.

In some areas of the country, children still make May Day baskets and hang them on doorknobs of homes in their neighborhood. Help children design a simple basket (a cone made of rolled paper or a shoe box) with a sturdy handle (a strip of cardstock). You may want to fill it with some candy or other treats, but use this as an assessment when children write special messages for others on pieces of small, colorful paper. Can students recall past Words to Remember? What words of encouragement can they share with people in the community? How can they witness to their neighbors—what would be the most important things to share about Jesus? Students may want to bring the baskets home to share with their own neighbors or have a mini field trip and walk around the school's neighborhood to distribute the baskets there.

After you're done with Lesson 67 (or at the end of the unit), use an Easter egg with an arrow printed on it in black permanent marker as a spinner for a review game. As a whole class or in small groups, have students sit in a circle around an egg spinner. One person twists it like a top; everyone waits until it stops to see who it points to. It will be that student's turn to answer a review question about an Easter story.

It's baseball season! Divide your students into two teams and play Bible baseball with the following questions, allowing students to advance around the "bases" (chairs in your classroom) and score, according to the difficulty level of the questions. Be sure to give everyone in your class a turn to answer a question (be "up to bat").

Single:

What did the women go to the tomb to do on Easter morning? (Put spices on Jesus' body)

Whom did the women meet at the tomb? (Angel)

Did the disciples believe the women when they said Jesus was alive again? (No)

What did the Emmaus disciples do when they realized they saw Jesus risen from the dead? (Ran to tell the other disciples) Bonus to make it a double: What city did they run back to? (Jerusalem)

What did Tabitha do for others? (Sew cloaks)

Who raised Tabitha from the dead with the Holy Spirit's power? (Peter)

Who was coming after Paul to kill him? (The Jewish people) Bonus to make it a double: Why? (Paul was preaching that Jesus is the Son of God.)

How did Paul's followers get him out of the city / in what did they hide him? (Basket that was lowered through a hole in the city wall)

What was on the disciples' heads at Pentecost? (Tongues of fire) Bonus to make it a double: What did that show? (They had received the gift of the Holy Spirit.)

What did the disciples hear right before the Holy Spirit came? (A sound like a rushing wind) Bonus to make a double: When everyone heard the sound, what did all the other people in the city do? (Met together in the outer courts of the temple)

When the disciples received the Holy Spirit, what were they able to do that they couldn't do before? (Speak in other languages)

Double:

Who did Mary think Jesus was when she first saw Him near the tomb? (Gardener)

When did the Emmaus disciples realize they were with Jesus? (When He broke the bread at the house)

What was Jesus' promise at His ascension? ("I will be with you always.")

At Jesus' ascension, He said that He would give His disciples a gift. How would they receive power? (When the Holy Spirit comes on them.) Bonus to make it a triple: Power to do what? (Be His witnesses where they live and all over the world)

What were the names of Timothy's mother and grandmother? (Eunice and Lois) Bonus to make it a triple: What was the name of the city they lived in? (Lystra)

What were Paul and Timothy partners in doing together? (They both preached God's Word/the Gospel; they wrote letters to churches.) Bonus to make it a triple: To which congregation—which city—were they both pastors? (Ephesus)

Triple:

What did Mary call Jesus when she realized He wasn't the gardener? (Teacher Or Rabboni)

What was the name of the disciple who went on the first missionary journey with Paul? (Barnabas) Bonus to make it a home run: When did Paul and Barnabas first meet? (When Barnabas defended Paul in Jerusalem and told the other disciples to trust him)

The name *Tabitha* means "gazelle" or "small deer." Do students think that's fitting because of what they know about how loving and caring she was? If necessary, explain that a deer is graceful and light footed. It seems that Tabitha was light on her feet, keeping busy serving many people through her sewing projects. Which animals were the other characters in this unit like? Can students think of their own comparisons? If not, provide some examples and see if they can make a match:

The women: Perhaps golden retriever dogs because they were loyal to Jesus, coming to His tomb to properly bury Him.

Peter: Perhaps a Chihuahua dog because of his impulsiveness and excitement as he ran to Jesus' tomb to find out what happened.

The disciples: Perhaps laughing hyenas because they didn't believe the women.

Emmaus disciples: Perhaps cheetahs because as soon as they recognized Jesus, they ran back to Jerusalem to tell the other disciples what had happened.

Mary Magdalene: Perhaps a cat because she wanted to stay by Jesus, just like a cat wants to curl up on your lap. But then when Jesus told her to tell the disciples, she leapt into action like a cat.

Paul: Perhaps a scary bear because he hurt the Christians, but then a warm, cuddly teddy bear because he became their friends. He still was a big, burly, noticeable figure in the Church. He was also tough, enduring a lot of pain, and was hunted like a bear can be.

Timothy: Perhaps a parrot because he was a loyal companion to the seafaring Paul, and he also was talkative about Jesus as he shared God's Word. He probably repeated some of the same phrases he heard Paul say.

Tabitha: Perhaps a busy beaver because she did many good works and accomplished many things to benefit the Church.

Ask your students what kind of animal *they* are most like, especially when it comes to sharing Jesus' love. Have them write down their response. They could even paint their faces like that animal or use a media-editing software program to superimpose their own head on the body of their animal; post the pictures in the hallway. If anyone asks about their faces or pictures, practice with your students what they can say.

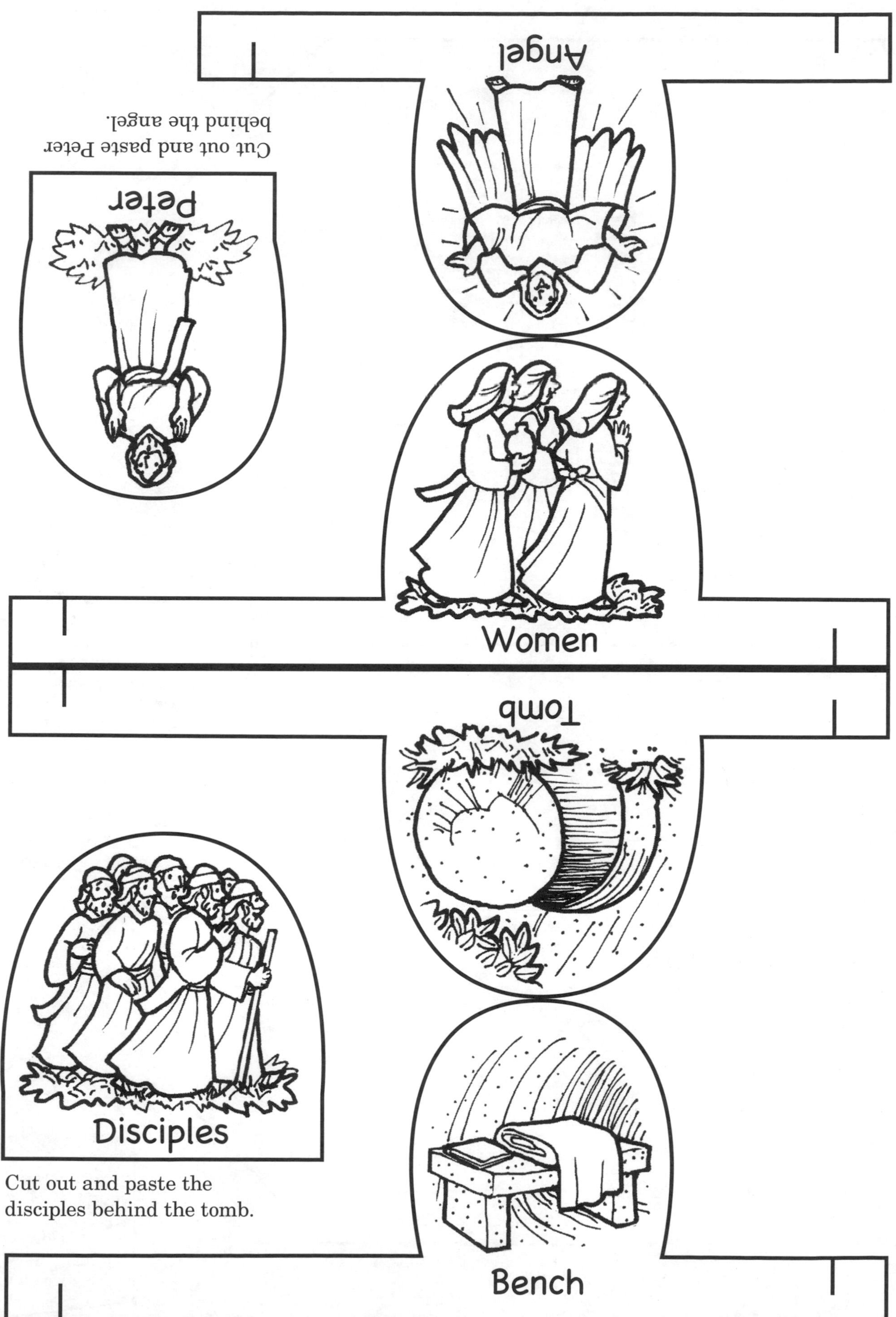
Angel
Cut out and paste Peter
behind the angel.
Peter
Women
Tomb
Disciples
Cut out and paste the
disciples behind the tomb.
Bench

Happy Easter!
I know
that my
Redeemer
lives.
Job 19:2
Love,

Your word is a lamp to my feet

and a light to my path. Psalm 119:105

Reminder of Jesus' Promise

¡Jesús es el Señor!

The Jewish People

Paul

Paul's followers

Barnabas

Jesus' followers

1
2
3
4

Month of ________________

Holy Spirit, help me show Jesus' love so all will know. Amen.

Sunday	Monday	Tuesday	Wednesday	Thursday	Friday	Saturday
	Call a grandparent			Draw someone a picture		Pick up your toys
Help with yard work		Smile at people in the store			Feed your pet	Send someone a card
	Clean your room		Eat your fruits and veggies		Compliment someone	
Dust the living room		Text someone		Set the table		
	Wipe marks off wall in your house		Water the plants			

"Sew" now what?

God Is with Me

(Maya, pronounced MY-uh, is sighing and pacing back and forth, clearly nervous about the first day of school. Jack comes up from behind her.)

Jack: *(boisterous, with a big slap on Maya's back)* Hiya, Maya! What's up?

Maya: *(jumping out of her skin)* Oh! Hi, Jack. You scared me. *(hangs her head)* I . . . I'm just trying to be happy about the first day of school, but . . . but it's not working.

Jack: Not working? It's great to see everybody again, isn't it? I can't wait for school to start again! First grade's going to be so much fun.

Maya: *(not convinced)* I . . . I hope so.

Jack: Don't worry, Maya. Remember what you taught me last year? When you're feeling scared or worried, just talk to Jesus! I still remember that you told me Jesus is our best friend and that He's with us all the time.

Maya: You're right, Jack. Thanks for reminding me. I was trying so hard to be happy, but it wasn't working. I just kept thinking of how nervous I was about first grade.

Jack: Last year we learned that the Bible tells us Jesus is with us always. Even though we can't see Him, we're never alone. He takes care of us.

Maya: Remember that picture we saw last year of Jesus holding the cute, little lamb? I kind of like thinking that Jesus is our Good Shepherd, watching over us. It makes me feel better.

Jack: Well, I liked the story about when Jesus went up to heaven.

Maya: Oh, yeah. When He ashy . . . ashend . . .

Jack: Ascended?

Maya: Yeah. Ascended up to heaven. Why does that story make you feel better?

Jack: Because Jesus promised His disciples that He would give them the Holy Spirit. The Holy Spirit is living in my heart. He gives me power. *(flexing his muscles and getting louder each time)* Power! Power! Power! *(Maya, still a little timid, jumps back each time Jack spits out the word* power.*)*

Maya: Ja-a-ack! *(You may want to add a comment like, "Settle down," "Chill out," or whatever you hear students saying to each other.)*

Jack: Sorry. I got a little carried away. But I just don't want you to be scared about school. You're the one who taught me that if Jesus loves us so much that He died on the cross for us, to forgive us from our sins, of course He'll love us and care for us each day.

Maya: You're right, Jack. I should have remembered. I . . . I think I'm starting to get excited about first grade. I think I might actually like it. And no matter what happens, Jesus is with me.

At this point, bring the puppets out into the classroom to meet the children. Tell the children to approach Maya gently so she won't get frightened. Ask the children to tell what they are excited about and what they think they will do or learn in first grade. Ad lib for the puppets, having them respond individually to each child's greetings, helping the children in your class to feel welcome and eager to be in first grade.

Sitting Still

Call the children together for worship. Give them time to recognize and respond to the call for worship. When they have all gathered in the worship center, begin in the name of the Father, Son, and Holy Spirit. Use the puppets to present this skit on appropriate behavior in worship. *(Maya approaches Jack, who sits with bowed head and folded hands, praying.)*

Maya: Jack! Hey! Jack! Want to sit together at chapel?

Jack: *(looks up briefly, then bows head again)* Shhh!

Maya: Oops! *(whispering loudly)* Sorry, Jack. *(waits quietly until Jack raises his head)* I didn't realize you were praying.

Jack: Oh, that's okay. Thanks for waiting 'til I was done. I just thought I'd better pray for help being good at chapel.

Maya: Why? What do you mean?

Jack: Well, I just have a hard time sitting still. My feet start swinging back and forth without me even thinking about it. And then sometimes I feel like I've been sitting for a million years and I just have to stretch my legs, but then when I push my feet up against the [chair, pew] of the people in front of me, they turn around and give me a mean look. I don't try to bother them . . . it just happens!

Maya: I know what you mean. Sometimes chapel seems so long to me too. I get tempted to start thinking about other things, like the cut on my finger or what I'm going to do at recess or someone's cute, sparkly shoes. Then I don't even hear what Pastor says!

Jack: Yeah. It's hard to be good the whole time at chapel. I know I want to be there to listen to what God has to say to us in His Word, the Bible. And I like to sing to God and praise Him. But sometimes my body has other ideas about what it wants to do. It's like I just can't help it!

Maya: So . . . what did you exactly say to God? I mean . . . how did you pray to be good in chapel?

Jack: Oh, I just said something like "Dear God, help me to be a good listener in chapel. Help me to be able to sit still and not bother other people. Thanks for Your Word that helps me learn about Jesus." That was about it. Why?

Maya: Oh, I was just wondering . . . 'cuz I should probably pray it too.

Tell the children, **We *all* can ask God to take away any temptations we might have not to listen to His Word.** Talk about how you can remove distractions while praying by bowing your head and closing your eyes. Then pray together, **Dear God, thank You for this special time to worship You. Help us to gladly listen to Your Word and sing Your praises, joyfully receiving Your gifts. Give us quiet hands and feet, ears to hear, and eyes to see Jesus. When we fail to worship in the right way, forgive us for Jesus' sake. Amen.**

Searching for Songs

(Hide Maya behind an object. Jack is in the foreground.)

Maya: *(peeking out, then immediately going back "undercover")* Psst!

(Jack turns his head both ways, looking around, but sees no one.)

Maya: Psst! Jack!

Jack: Who's there? Who said that?

Maya: *(from behind the object)* Me.

Jack: Me who? Where are you?

Maya: *(sneaking out, whispering)* It's me, Maya.

Jack: Maya, what in the world are you doing, sneaking around like this?

(If possible, Maya has a hymnal or songbook, whatever your school typically uses for chapel.)

Maya: Well, I'm a little embarrassed. *(looking around to see that no one else is listening)*

I don't know how to find the songs in the hymnal [songbook]. I don't want to look dumb when we go to chapel. I figured that since you're so good at math, maybe you could show me how it works.

Jack: Well, sure, Maya. I'd be glad to help. But you don't need to feel bad. I'm sure a lot of people don't know how to look things up. And last year, we had fifth-grade chapel buddies, so they always helped us, but this year we'll be on our own.

Maya: So what do I do? What if Pastor says, "Turn to hymn number 817?"

Jack: Well, first of all, you could maybe guess that since it's in the 800s, it will be toward the back, since that's such a high number. It will be a three-digit number, since it's a hundreds number.

Maya: So if it's *eight* hundred seventeen, where will the eight be, again?

Jack: The eight will be the first number. Flip through the one hundreds, two hundreds, three hundreds, and all of the pages until you get to the eight hundreds, with the eight in the hundreds place, the number farthest to the left. *(If possible, have Jack flip through the hymnal or songbook. If using* All God's People Sing, *you may also want to show the children how the hymns are in alphabetical order.)*

Maya: And then what?

Jack: Then look for the number 17. It will have a number 1 in the tens place and a number 7 in the ones place, the number farthest to the right.

Maya: So the order of the numbers is an 8, then a 1, and then a 7?

Jack: Yep! That's all there is to it. You wanna hear a little secret I learned?

Maya: Yeah! Sure. What do you do?

Jack: Well, if I'm finding it by myself, I secretly look at the person next to me to see what the number looks like and how far back in the hymnal it is. They don't even know I'm watching them, and I don't even ask them for help, but just looking at how they did it helps me! So remember, Maya, it's okay to ask someone for help. But if you want to try it yourself, just watch how other people do it.

Maya: You think it will work? You really think I can do it?

Jack: Sure, you can!

Maya: Thanks for teaching me. Now I don't feel so silly anymore. Now I can think about Jesus and not have to think so hard about what to do during worship. *(whispering)* Bye! *(Maya sneaks away, back the way she came.)*

God's Word Is to Be Heard

(Jack comes out holding a small pillow. Maya turns, questioningly.)

Maya: Um, Jack . . . what are you doing with a pillow?

Jack: I think I've got a great new idea!

Maya: But it's almost time for worship. You're not planning on falling asleep, are you? I know sometimes when we go to church, pastor's sermons can get pretty long, but I don't think that's very nice to actually draw attention to the fact that you're not planning on listening.

Jack: No, no. It's the opposite of that. I *do* plan to pay attention to God's Word.

Maya: Okay. I don't get it.

Jack: You know how [your name] is always telling us to respect God's Word? Well, I thought of a great way to take care of the Bible . . . setting it down on top of a soft pillow. That way it won't get hurt. Isn't that a great way to show how much I love the Bible?

Maya: Uh, Jack . . . I don't think that's what . . .

Jack: *(interrupting, excitedly)* My mom's always telling me to take care of my toys. Like the collector race car that I got from Uncle Matt . . . it's so special that my mom doesn't even let me play with it or take it out of the box. It just sits on top of my shelf so it won't get hurt. So I figured that the Bible is even more special than that, so it has to have something to protect it. Hey, I think I just made a new invention . . . a Bible cushion. Cool, huh? What do you think?

Maya: Well, I, uh . . .

Jack: *(interrupting again, pretending to sound like a commercial)* The amazing Bible cushion. A great new way to respect God's Word . . .

Maya: *(interrupting)* Jack . . .

Jack: Comes in many assorted colors like Bible blue or Noah's rainbow . . .

Maya: *(interrupting)* Jack . . .

Jack: Comes in many different sizes, like . . .

Maya: *(interrupting, yelling)* JACK! *(Jack looks startled. He finally stops talking and looks at Maya. Maya puts her arm around Jack and talks in a quiet voice.)* Jack, I don't want to hurt your feelings. You have the right idea about respecting God's Word. But when [your name] says that, [he/she] means that we *should* use it. The Bible shouldn't just sit on a shelf so it doesn't get ruined. In fact, you know what?

Jack: What?

Maya: My mom even lets me write in my Bible. I can underline verses that I really like, or draw pictures on the side of the page. She said she might even get me a highlighter to color over the words.

Jack: No way! She lets you do that? Aren't you destroying your Bible? When I dropped the Bible the other day in church, my mom gave me a mean look. I figured she was mad that I wasn't taking care of it.

Maya: I bet she was just mad about the loud noise you made during church. I doubt that she was mad you were reading it. The way to respect God's Word is to read it and to hear it. If you don't ever use the Bible, you're not showing that you love it.

Jack: So you're telling me that I should sell bookmarks and pencils for Bibles, not pillows?

Maya: That would be a lot better. God's Word is so special because it's how we learn about how much God loves us. He loved us so much that He sent His Son to die on the cross to forgive our sins. We shouldn't just let that Good News sit on a shelf. There are a lot of neat stories in the Bible!

Jack: I know! [your name] said that the Bible is how God talks to us. That's why it's called God's Word. It's like God speaking to us. He told the people what to write and they wrote it. Even though they wrote the stories a long time ago, it's what we need to hear today.

Maya: You understood that part of it!

Jack: I may not have known *how* to respect the Bible, but I at least knew *why*.

Maya: So now what are you going to do with your pillow?

Jack: I guess I'll just have to sit on it. It will make me comfortable, so I can sit and listen to God's Word for a looong time.

Psalm 24

Print the word *psalm* on the board and explain, **A psalm is a song to God in the Bible.** Hold up a Bible opened to the very center and say, **The psalms are easy to find. There are 150 of them in the very center of the Bible.** Have the children imitate your motions as you read portions of Psalm 24 (NIV).

The earth is the LORD's, and everything in it, *(sweep arms in a wide circle)* **the world, and all who live in it;** *(point to individuals)*

For He founded it upon the seas and established it upon the waters. *(make wavy water motions)*

Who may ascend the hill of the LORD? Who may stand in His holy place? *(point up high)*

He who has clean hands and a pure heart, *(place both hands over heart)* **who does not lift up his soul to an idol or swear by what is false.** *(move head and hand to indicate* no*)*

He will receive blessing from the LORD and vindication from God his Savior. *(make the sign of the cross)*

On the remaining verses, indicate number 1 with a raised index finger whenever you say *LORD*, place up-stretched fingers beside your head to form a crown whenever you say *King*, and lift your arms on the word *glory*.

Lift up your heads, O you gates; be lifted up, you ancient doors, that the King *(crown)* **of glory** *(lift arms)* **may come in.**

Who is this King *(crown)* **of glory** *(lift arms)***? The LORD** *(#1)* **strong and mighty, the LORD** *(#1)* **mighty in battle.**

Lift up your heads, O you gates; lift them up, you ancient doors, that the King *(crown)* **of glory** *(lift arms)* **may come in.**

Who is He, this King *(crown)* **of glory** *(lift arms)***? The LORD** *(#1)* **Almighty—He is the King** *(crown)* **of glory** *(lift arms)***.**

Ask, **Why can we call God the *King of creation*?** (He made the world and still preserves the things in it.) Reread Psalm 24:1. **We praise and thank God for all the blessings He has given.** Continue, **We call God the *King of creation*. We also call Him the *King of glory*. How did God show that Jesus is the King of glory, even when Jesus was a tiny baby?** (Angels announced His birth; Wise Men came to worship the newborn King; He fulfilled the prophecies of the promised Savior King.) Then reread Psalm 24:4. Point out that none of us can do this perfectly. We use our hands to do wrong things; our hearts are sinful; we do not always obey God's will. That is why Jesus, the King of glory, entered our world, and on Palm Sunday entered Jerusalem, so that He could die on the cross to take away our sins. **Pilate placed a sign above Jesus' head on the cross. It said Jesus was the King of the Jews. But Jesus is much more. He is the King of glory, who rules over heaven and earth!**

Psalm 95

Say, **Today we will hear another psalm that talks about God as our King. But this psalm gives us two other pictures. One is of God as a shepherd. A shepherd takes care of his sheep. We are like a flock of sheep because God takes care of us. The other picture the psalm uses is of God as a rock. Can you think of a way that God and a rock are alike?** (Both are strong.) **Let's learn more about Psalm 95—a song of praise to God.**

Say, **Psalm 95 begins by telling the main reason we praise God. We praise God because of salvation. Do you remember a shorter word that begins with the same sound and means the same as *salvation*?** (Saved) **How did Jesus save us?** (By dying on the cross to take away our sins) **Why did Jesus save us?** (Because He loves us and wants to take us to heaven someday) **Let's praise the Lord!** Have the children imitate your motions as you say the psalm.

Come, *(make a beckoning motion)* **let us sing for joy to the LORD; let us shout aloud** *(cup hands around mouth)* **to the Rock** *(pound one fisted hand onto the open palm of other hand)* **of our salvation.** *(make the sign of the cross)*

Let us come before Him with thanksgiving *(fold hands)* **and [praise] Him with music and song.** *(pretend to strum a guitar or play a piano)*

For the LORD is the great God, *(lift arms in a wide-sweeping gesture)* **the great King above all gods.** *(point upward)*

In His hand are the depths of the earth, *(reach low)* **and the mountain peaks belong to Him.** *(touch fingertips to make mountain shapes)*

The sea is His, for He made it, *(make wavy motions)* **and His hands formed the dry land.** *(pretend to mold clay)*

Come, let us bow down in worship, *(bow from the waist)* **let us kneel before the LORD our Maker;** *(kneel)*

for He is our God and we are the people of His pasture, the flock under His care. *(give yourself a hug)*

God Blesses Us

Psalm 24:1, 7–10

The earth is the  's, and everything in it, the world, and all who live in it. …

Lift up your heads, O you gates; be lifted up, you ancient doors, that the of may come in.

Who is this of ?

The strong and mighty, the mighty in battle.

Lift up your heads, O you gates; lift them up, you ancient doors, that the of may come in.

Who is He, this of ?

The Almighty—He is the of .

Psalm 95:1–7

1. Come, let us  for joy to the LORD;

   Let us  aloud to the 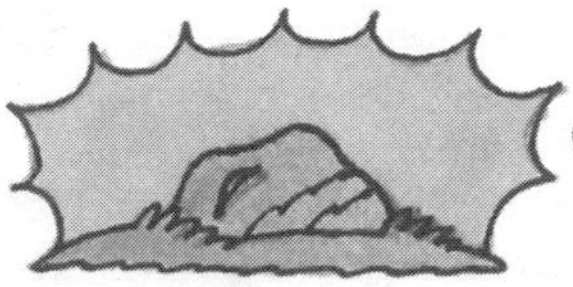 of our salvation.

2. Let us come before Him with thanksgiving

   and [praise] Him with  and song.

3. For the LORD is the great God, the great  above all gods.

4. In His  are the depths of the " ",

   and the  peaks belong to Him.

5. The  is His, for He made it,

   and His  formed the dry 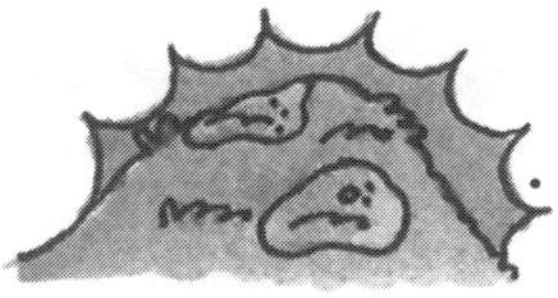 .

6. Come, let us  down in worship,

   let us  before the LORD our Maker;

7. For He is our God and we are the  of His pasture,

   the  under His care.

Psalm 148

Read aloud the portions of Psalm 148 on the Reproducible Page. Then ask, What word did you hear over and over again? (Praise) Tell the children that you will read the psalm again. Every time they hear the word praise, they are to "explode" out of their chairs (meaning they jump up with raised arms and then sit down again).

Assign children to be the parts of creation mentioned in the psalm. For example, one individual or small group can be sea creatures, someone else can be lightning and hail, and so on. Tell the children that when they hear their part of creation mentioned in the psalm, they are to jump up and shout, "Praise the Lord!" Use copies of the Reproducible Page to write a new psalm together. Choose elements of creation not mentioned in Psalm 148 and print them in the blanks (according to categories listed in parentheses). On the board, print the words suggested by the children so that spelling does not become an issue or obstacle. Use your completed psalm, reading it together to praise God.

Psalm 150

Use the Jack and Maya puppets. If possible, have Maya hold a small Bible.

Maya: Hey, Jack. Today we are going to hear Psalm 150. Listen to these great words: "Praise God in His sanctuary." *Sanctuary* means "the church."

Jack: I know that.

Maya: And then it says, "Praise Him in His mighty heavens."

Jack: So it's saying we can praise God *in* church and also everywhere *out* of church.

Maya: Right, inside and outside. *(Hold Maya curled up tight on the word* inside *and hold her stretched wide on the word* outside.*)*

Jack: And when I think of *church* I think of a lot of "ups and downs," like stand up, sit down, stand up, sit down.

Maya: Oh, Jack. You are so silly.

Jack: Actually, this *in* and *out* and *up* and *down* makes me think of a song that praises God! Let's sing "Happy All the Time" (*LOSP*, p. 59).

Then tell the children that you are going to read the psalm that Maya was talking about. Say, **Here are three things to listen for: (1) each verse says the word *praise* at least two times; (2) the psalm writer asks all the instruments in the whole orchestra to join in praising God; and (3) at the end he asks the whole choir—everything that has breath—to praise the Lord.** (Explain that a *lyre* is a handheld harp.) Read aloud Psalm 150 from a Bible. On the Reproducible Page, see how many of the instruments the children can identify. Point out the old and new style of trumpets, harps, and flutes. The instruments used in Bible times are the tambourine, shofar (ram's horn), trumpet, flute, and lyre (harp).

Praise the Lord!

(Psalm 148)

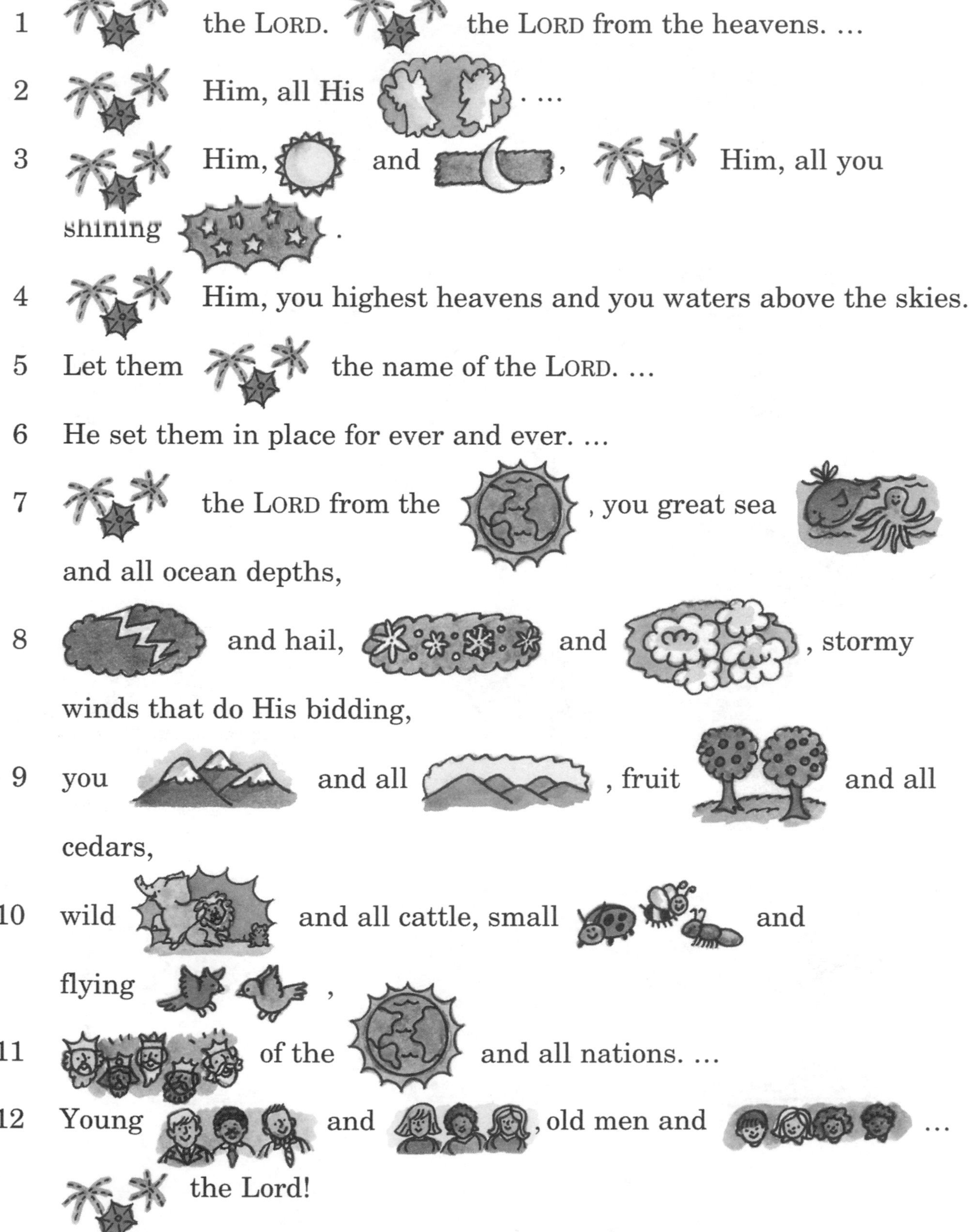

1 the LORD. the LORD from the heavens. …

2 Him, all His . …

3 Him, and , Him, all you

shining .

4 Him, you highest heavens and you waters above the skies.

5 Let them the name of the LORD. …

6 He set them in place for ever and ever. …

7 the LORD from the , you great sea

and all ocean depths,

8 and hail, and , stormy

winds that do His bidding,

9 you and all , fruit and all

cedars,

10 wild and all cattle, small and

flying ,

11 of the and all nations. …

12 Young and , old men and …

the Lord!

Praise with Instruments and Choirs (Psalm 150)

Can you name some of these instruments? Can you circle the ones that may have been used in Bible times? Place an X next to instruments you have heard used in church to praise the Lord.

Prayers

Use this responsive prayer. Practice the children's words, "Father, we thank Thee," before using the prayer.

Teacher: For flowers that bloom about our feet,

Children: Father, we thank Thee.

T: For tender grass so fresh, so sweet,

C: Father, we thank Thee.

T: For the song of bird and hum of bee, For all things fair we hear or see,

C: Father in heaven, we thank Thee.

T: For blue of stream and blue of sky,

C: Father, we thank Thee.

T: For pleasant shade of branches high,

C: Father, we thank Thee.

T: For fragrant air and cooling breeze, For beauty of the blooming trees,

C: Father in heaven, we thank Thee.

T: For this new morning with its light,

C: Father, we thank Thee.

T: For rest and shelter of the night,

C: Father, we thank Thee.

T: For health and food, for love and friends, For everything Thy goodness sends,

C: Father in heaven, we thank Thee.

Author Unknown

Good morning, dear Jesus,
This day is for You.
I give to You all
That I think, say, and do. Amen.

All through the day,
I humbly pray,
O be my Guard and Guide:
My sins forgive
And let me live,
Dear Jesus near Your side. Amen.

Dear Jesus, bless my friends today
And all my family too.
Teach me to show my love to them
In everything I do. Amen.

Praise God, from whom all blessings flow;
Praise Him, all creatures here below;
Praise Him above, ye heavenly host:
Praise Father, Son, and Holy Ghost. Amen.

(*LSB* 805)

As you prepare to use the following prayer, tell the children they will be thanking God for different things. Have them volunteer items beforehand or make this a circle prayer. Allow children to mention three or four items each time you pause. Then go on to the next paragraph of thanksgiving. Be sure the children understand the directions before you begin praying. Practicing one or two paragraphs first may help.

Dear Jesus, thank You for today. You are so good to us. Thank You for what we had for breakfast this morning. For *(pause for the children's words)*.

Thank You, Jesus, for the things we saw on our way to school today. For *(pause for the children's words)*.

Thank You for our classroom and for all the things You've given us to use each day. For *(pause for the children's words)*.

Thank You for our friends, Jesus, to play with and to have fun with. For *(pause for the children's words)*.

We also thank You for other things that You have given us. For *(pause for the children's words)*.

Thank You most of all for giving us Yourself, Jesus, for dying on the cross for us, and for telling us of Your love in Your Book, the Bible. Amen.

God, Whose Name is Love

Sometimes

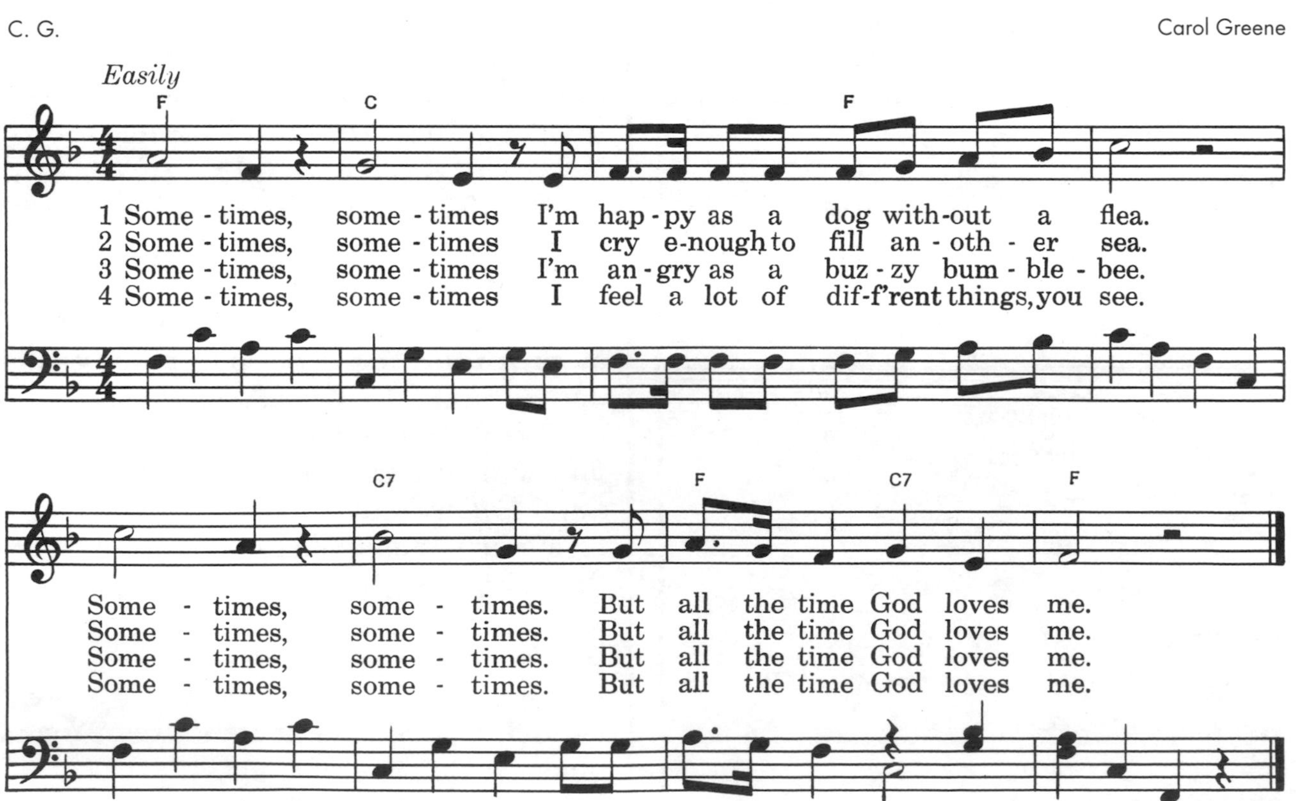

The Friendly Beasts

12th Century English

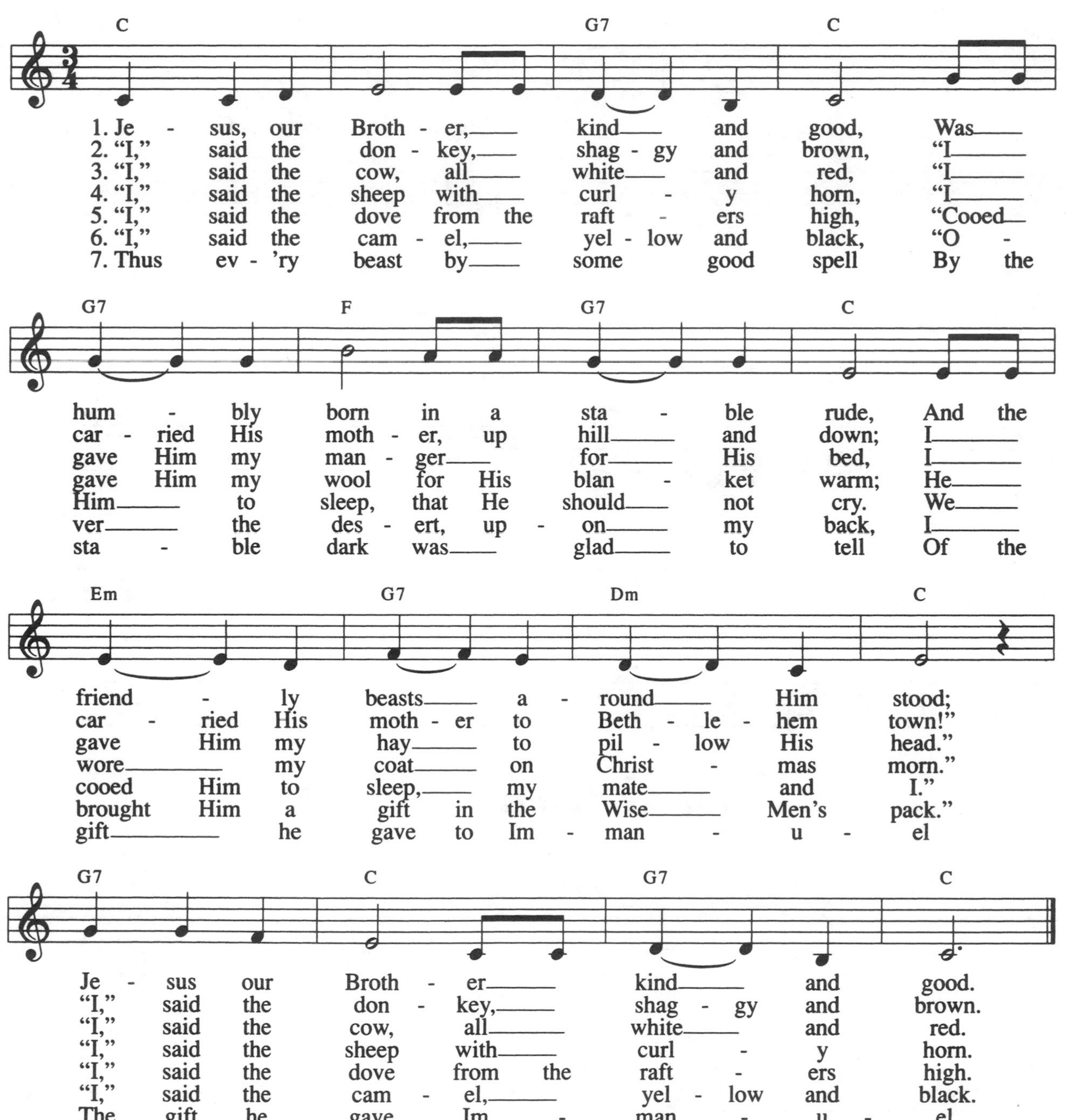

(Have children make animal masks to wear when singing this song or take the part of the animals mentioned as they act out the stanzas.)

My Savior Lives

Carol Greene | L. V. Beethoven, adapted

Happily

My Sav - ior lives! My Sav - ior lives! He loves me so and al - ways stays be - side me. My Sav - ior lives! My Sav - ior lives! I take His hand, for He will al - ways guide me.

I Am Jesus' Helper

Thanks to Jesus We Will Sing

Robert Louis Stevenson, alt. J. Battishill

Jesus, We Thank You

Wihelmina D' Arcy Stephens, alt. Grace Wilbur Conant

The Morning Bright

T. D. Summers, 1845

English melody

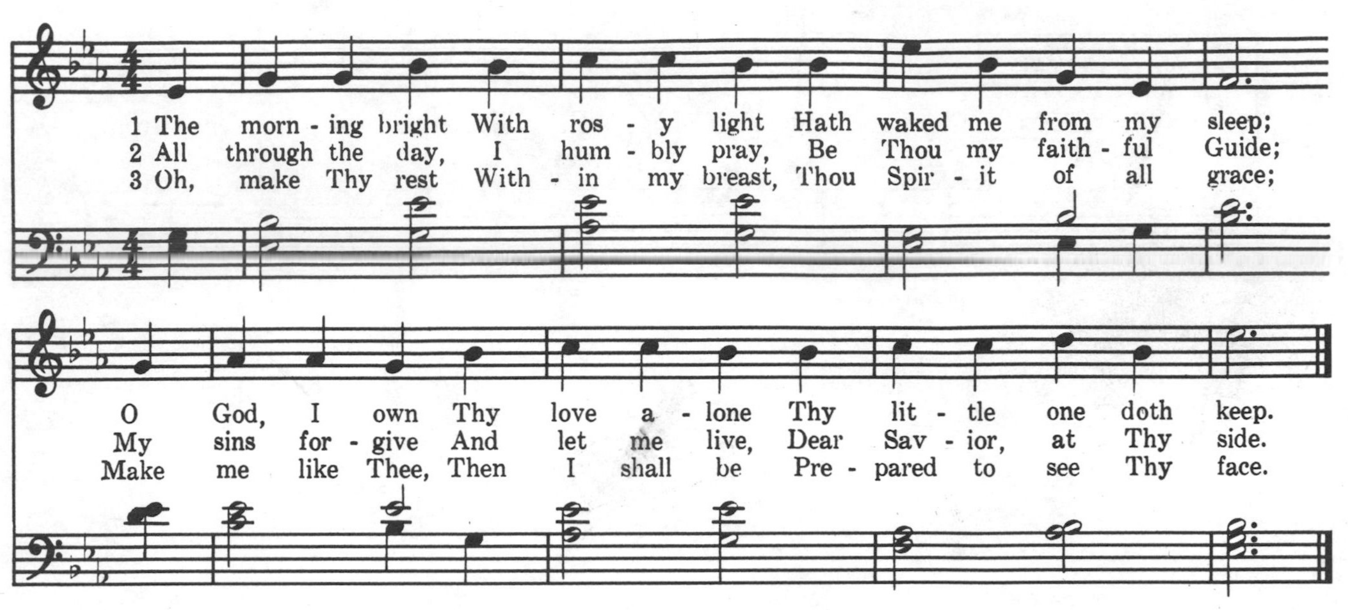

God Is There

Carol Greene

Early American Hymn

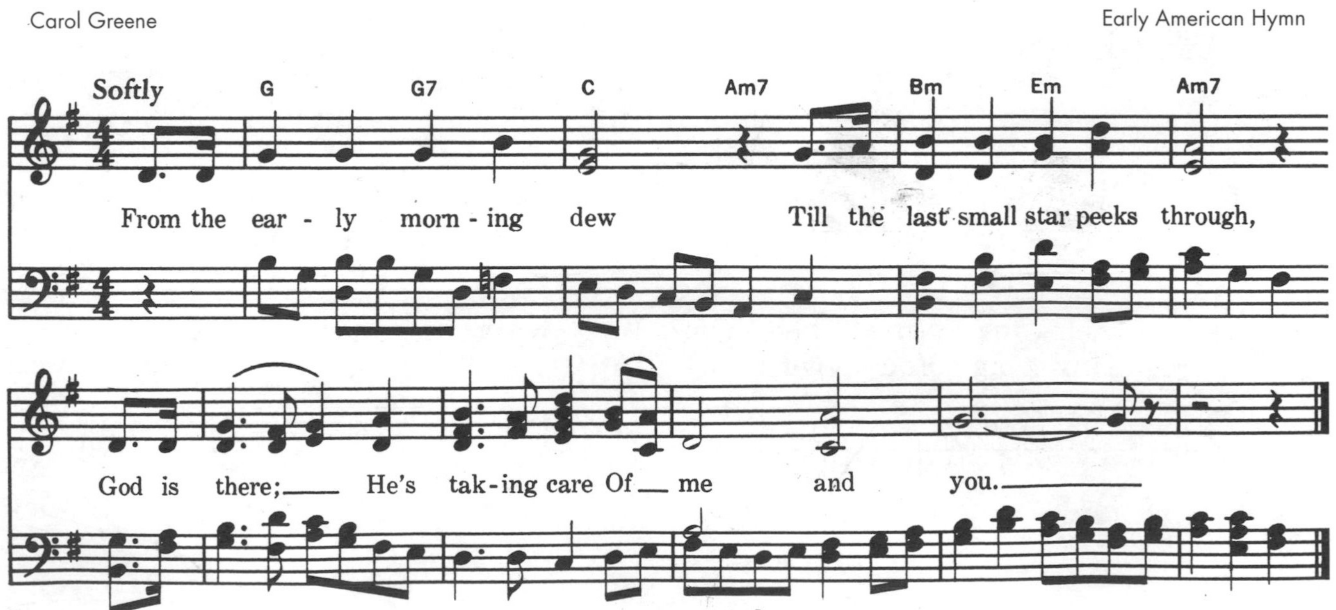